# 77 Polish Recipes for Home

By: Kelly Johnson

# Table of Contents

Traditional Polish Dishes:

- Pierogi (Polish Dumplings)
- Bigos (Hunter's Stew)
- Zurek (Sour Rye Soup)
- Golabki (Cabbage Rolls)
- Kielbasa and Kapusta (Sausage with Sauerkraut)
- Placki Ziemniaczane (Potato Pancakes)
- Rosół (Chicken Broth)
- Kotlet Schabowy (Pork Cutlet)
- Zrazy (Beef Rolls)
- Barszcz (Beet Soup)

Polish Soups:

- Kapuśniak (Cabbage Soup)
- Zupa Grzybowa (Mushroom Soup)
- Zupa Ogórkowa (Cucumber Soup)
- Zupa Pomidorowa (Tomato Soup)
- Grochówka (Pea Soup)
- Krem z Kalafiora (Cream of Cauliflower Soup)
- Chłodnik (Cold Beet Soup)
- Zupa Kalafiorowa (Cauliflower Soup)
- Zupa Buraczkowa (Beetroot Soup)
- Zupa Serowa (Cheese Soup)

Polish Appetizers:

- Paszteciki (Puff Pastry with Fillings)
- Rolmopsy (Herring Rolls)
- Śledź w Oleju (Herring in Oil)
- Kabanosy (Thin Smoked Sausages)
- Sałatka Jarzynowa (Polish Vegetable Salad)
- Jajka Faszerowane (Stuffed Eggs)
- Placki Ziemniaczane z Lososiem (Potato Pancakes with Salmon)
- Tatar (Beef Tartare)
- Zakąski (Appetizer Platter)

- Naleśniki z Serem (Cheese-filled Crepes)

Polish Main Courses:

- Ryba po Grecku (Fish Greek Style)
- Kurczak Pieczony (Roast Chicken)
- Placek Ziemniaczany
- Jagnięcina Pieczona (Roast Lamb)
- Karp smażony (Fried Carp)
- Kaczka Pieczona (Roast Duck)
- Pieczeń Wieprzowa (Roast Pork)
- Kurczak duszony w Piwie (Beer-Braised Chicken)
- Pieczony Indyk (Roast Turkey)
- Cielecina duszona z Warzywami (Veal Stew)

Polish Side Dishes:

- Kasza Gryczana (Buckwheat Groats)
- Placki Ziemniaczane z Gulaszem (Potato Pancakes with Goulash)
- Kopytka (Potato Dumplings)
- Ziemniaki Puree (Mashed Potatoes)
- Kluski Śląskie (Silesian Dumplings)
- Kiszona Kapusta (Pickled Cabbage)
- Kasza Manna (Semolina Porridge)
- Kopytka (Potato Dumplings)
- Kiszony Ogórek (Pickles)
- Marchewka z Groszkiem (Carrots with Peas)

Polish Desserts:

- Sernik (Cheesecake)
- Makowiec (Poppy Seed Roll)
- Kremówka Papieska (Papal Cream Cake)
- Pączki (Polish Doughnuts)
- Babka (Easter Cake)
- Placuszki z Jabłkami (Apple Pancakes)
- Ciasto Drożdżowe z Owocami (Yeast Cake with Fruit)
- Kompot z Suszu (Dried Fruit Compote)
- Chałka (Sweet Bread)
- Ciasto Kruche z Owocami (Shortcrust Pastry with Fruit)

Polish Breads:

- Chleb Wiejski (Country Bread)
- Bułki Płatki Owsiane (Oat Rolls)
- Chleb Razowy (Rye Bread)
- Chałka (Sweet Bread)
- Bułki Pyszne (Delicious Rolls)
- Bułki z Makiem (Poppy Seed Rolls)
- Chleb Pszenno-Zytni (Wheat-Rye Bread)
- Bułki Drożdżowe (Yeast Rolls)
- Chleb Ziemniaczany (Potato Bread)
- Bułki Cynamonowe (Cinnamon Rolls)

Polish Beverages:

- Kompot Owocowy (Fruit Compote)
- Kisiel (Fruit Jelly)
- Wódka (Vodka)
- Herbata (Tea)
- Kawa (Coffee)
- Kefir (Fermented Milk Drink)
- Piwo (Beer)

# Traditional Polish Dishes:

**Pierogi (Polish Dumplings)**

Ingredients:

*For the Dough:*

- 2 cups all-purpose flour
- 1 large egg
- 1/2 cup water (adjust as needed)
- 1/2 teaspoon salt

*For the Filling:*

- 3 cups mashed potatoes
- 1 cup farmer's cheese (or ricotta)
- 1 small onion, finely chopped and sautéed
- Salt and pepper to taste

Instructions:

*For the Dough:*

> In a large mixing bowl, combine the flour and salt. Make a well in the center and add the egg.
> Slowly incorporate the water into the flour, mixing continuously until the dough comes together.
> Knead the dough on a floured surface until it becomes smooth and elastic. Wrap it in plastic wrap and let it rest for at least 30 minutes.

*For the Filling:*

> Boil or bake the potatoes until fully cooked. Mash them in a large bowl.
> Add the farmer's cheese, sautéed onions, salt, and pepper to the mashed potatoes. Mix thoroughly.

*Assembly:*

> Roll out the dough on a floured surface until it is about 1/8 inch thick.

Use a round cookie cutter or a glass to cut out circles from the dough.
Place a small spoonful of the potato filling in the center of each dough circle.
Fold the dough in half to create a half-moon shape, then press the edges firmly to seal. You can use a fork to crimp the edges for a decorative touch.
Bring a large pot of salted water to a boil. Carefully drop the pierogi into the boiling water and cook until they float to the surface (about 3-5 minutes).
Remove the pierogi with a slotted spoon and place them on a plate.
Optional: Sauté the boiled pierogi in butter until they are lightly browned for added flavor.
Serve the pierogi warm with sour cream, sautéed onions, or your favorite sauce.

Enjoy these homemade Polish dumplings as a delightful and comforting dish that captures the essence of traditional Polish cuisine!

**Bigos (Hunter's Stew)**

Ingredients:

- 1 lb sauerkraut, drained and rinsed
- 1 lb fresh cabbage, shredded
- 1 lb mixed meats (such as kielbasa, bacon, pork shoulder, and beef stew meat), diced
- 1 large onion, chopped
- 2 cloves garlic, minced
- 2 bay leaves
- 1 teaspoon caraway seeds
- 1 teaspoon dried marjoram
- 1 teaspoon paprika
- Salt and pepper to taste
- 1 cup dried wild mushrooms, soaked in hot water and chopped
- 1 cup dry red wine
- 2 tablespoons tomato paste
- 1 tablespoon vegetable oil
- Water, as needed

Instructions:

In a large pot, heat the vegetable oil over medium heat. Add the diced meats and brown them on all sides.

Add the chopped onions and minced garlic to the pot. Sauté until the onions are translucent.

Stir in the tomato paste and cook for a few minutes until it starts to caramelize.

Pour in the red wine, scraping the bottom of the pot to release any flavorful bits. Allow the wine to reduce slightly.

Add the sauerkraut, shredded cabbage, caraway seeds, marjoram, paprika, bay leaves, and soaked, chopped mushrooms to the pot. Mix everything together.

Season with salt and pepper to taste. Be cautious with salt, as sauerkraut can be salty.

Pour enough water into the pot to cover the ingredients. Bring the mixture to a boil.

Reduce the heat to low, cover the pot, and let the stew simmer for at least 2-3 hours. The longer it cooks, the better the flavors meld.

Adjust the seasoning if needed. Remove the bay leaves before serving.

Serve the Bigos hot with crusty bread, boiled potatoes, or as desired.

Bigos is a dish that improves with time, so it's often made in advance and reheated. Enjoy this hearty and satisfying Hunter's Stew, a staple in Polish cuisine!

**Zurek (Sour Rye Soup)**

Ingredients:

*For the Sour Starter (Zakwas):*

- 1 cup rye flour
- 1 cup warm water

*For the Soup:*

- 6 cups chicken or vegetable broth
- 1 cup sourdough starter (zakwas)
- 1 cup cooked and diced Polish sausage (such as kielbasa)
- 1 cup diced cooked ham
- 1 large onion, finely chopped
- 2 cloves garlic, minced
- 2 medium carrots, diced
- 2 medium potatoes, peeled and diced
- 1 bay leaf
- 1 teaspoon caraway seeds
- 1 teaspoon dried marjoram
- Salt and pepper to taste
- 1 cup sour cream

*Optional Garnishes:*

- Hard-boiled eggs, sliced
- Fresh parsley, chopped

Instructions:

*For the Sour Starter (Zakwas):*

Mix the rye flour with warm water in a glass or ceramic bowl. Cover it loosely with a cloth and let it ferment at room temperature for 3-4 days. Stir it once a day.

When the mixture develops a sour smell, strain it through a fine mesh sieve, discarding any solids. The liquid is your sour starter (zakwas).

*For the Soup:*

In a large pot, combine the chicken or vegetable broth, sourdough starter (zakwas), diced sausage, diced ham, chopped onion, minced garlic, diced carrots, diced potatoes, bay leaf, caraway seeds, and dried marjoram.
Bring the mixture to a boil, then reduce the heat to low and let it simmer until the vegetables are tender (usually about 20-30 minutes).
Season the soup with salt and pepper to taste.
In a separate bowl, mix the sour cream until smooth. Gradually add a ladle of hot soup to the sour cream, stirring constantly. This helps to temper the sour cream and prevent curdling.
Gradually add the tempered sour cream mixture back into the soup, stirring well. Continue to simmer the soup for an additional 10-15 minutes to allow the flavors to meld.
Remove the bay leaf before serving.
Ladle the Sour Rye Soup into bowls and garnish with sliced hard-boiled eggs and chopped fresh parsley if desired.

Serve this flavorful and tangy Zurek with a slice of rye bread for an authentic and satisfying Polish dining experience.

**Golabki (Cabbage Rolls)**

Ingredients:

*For the Cabbage Rolls:*

- 1 large head of cabbage
- 1 lb ground pork or a mix of pork and beef
- 1 cup cooked rice
- 1 medium onion, finely chopped
- 1 clove garlic, minced
- 1 egg
- Salt and pepper to taste
- 1/2 teaspoon dried marjoram
- 1/2 teaspoon dried thyme

*For the Tomato Sauce:*

- 2 cups tomato sauce
- 1 cup beef or vegetable broth
- 1 tablespoon tomato paste
- 1 tablespoon sugar
- Salt and pepper to taste

Instructions:

Preheat the oven to 350°F (175°C).
Bring a large pot of water to a boil. Carefully immerse the whole head of cabbage into the boiling water. Boil for about 5-7 minutes, or until the outer leaves become soft and pliable. Remove the cabbage from the water and let it cool slightly. Gently peel off the softened cabbage leaves, being careful not to tear them. If the inner leaves are still too firm, return the cabbage to the boiling water for a few more minutes.
In a large mixing bowl, combine the ground meat, cooked rice, chopped onion, minced garlic, egg, marjoram, thyme, salt, and pepper. Mix until well combined. Place a spoonful of the meat and rice mixture in the center of each cabbage leaf. Fold in the sides and roll up the cabbage to encase the filling. Place the rolled cabbage leaves seam side down in a baking dish.

In a separate bowl, mix together the tomato sauce, beef or vegetable broth, tomato paste, sugar, salt, and pepper to create the sauce.

Pour the tomato sauce mixture over the cabbage rolls, ensuring they are well coated.

Cover the baking dish with foil and bake in the preheated oven for about 1 to 1.5 hours, or until the cabbage rolls are cooked through and the flavors meld.

Remove from the oven and let the Golabki rest for a few minutes before serving.

Serve the Golabki hot, drizzled with the tomato sauce, and accompanied by a dollop of sour cream if desired.

Enjoy these delicious and comforting Polish Cabbage Rolls as a main course for a hearty and satisfying meal!

**Kielbasa and Kapusta (Sausage with Sauerkraut)**

Ingredients:

- 1 lb kielbasa sausage, sliced into bite-sized pieces
- 1 large onion, thinly sliced
- 2 cloves garlic, minced
- 1 large can (about 28 oz) sauerkraut, drained and rinsed
- 1 tablespoon vegetable oil
- 1 teaspoon caraway seeds
- 1 bay leaf
- 1 cup chicken or vegetable broth
- Salt and pepper to taste
- Fresh parsley, chopped (for garnish, optional)

Instructions:

In a large skillet or Dutch oven, heat the vegetable oil over medium heat.
Add the sliced kielbasa to the skillet and brown on all sides. This should take about 5-7 minutes.
Once the kielbasa is browned, remove it from the skillet and set it aside.
In the same skillet, add the sliced onions and minced garlic. Sauté until the onions are soft and translucent.
Stir in the drained and rinsed sauerkraut, caraway seeds, and bay leaf. Cook for a few minutes to allow the flavors to meld.
Pour the chicken or vegetable broth over the sauerkraut mixture and bring it to a simmer.
Return the browned kielbasa to the skillet, nestling the pieces into the sauerkraut mixture.
Cover the skillet and let the dish simmer for about 20-30 minutes, allowing the flavors to meld and the sauerkraut to soften.
Season with salt and pepper to taste. Remove the bay leaf before serving.
Garnish with chopped fresh parsley if desired.

Serve Kielbasa and Kapusta hot, either as a standalone dish or over mashed potatoes or boiled potatoes. This savory and satisfying meal captures the essence of Polish comfort food.

## Placki Ziemniaczane (Potato Pancakes)

Ingredients:

- 4 large potatoes, peeled
- 1 small onion
- 1/4 cup all-purpose flour
- 2 large eggs
- 1 teaspoon salt
- 1/2 teaspoon black pepper
- Vegetable oil for frying
- Sour cream or applesauce for serving (optional)

Instructions:

Grate the potatoes using a box grater or a food processor. Place the grated potatoes in a clean kitchen towel or cheesecloth and squeeze out as much liquid as possible.

Finely grate the onion and add it to the grated potatoes.

In a large mixing bowl, combine the grated potatoes and onions with flour, eggs, salt, and black pepper. Mix well to form a batter.

In a large skillet, heat a generous amount of vegetable oil over medium-high heat. Spoon the potato batter into the hot oil, forming small pancakes. Flatten them slightly with the back of a spoon.

Fry the pancakes until the edges are golden brown, approximately 3-4 minutes on each side.

Once the potato pancakes are crispy and golden, transfer them to a plate lined with paper towels to absorb excess oil.

Continue the process until all the batter is used, adding more oil to the pan as needed.

Serve the Placki Ziemniaczane hot, optionally with a dollop of sour cream or applesauce on top.

Enjoy these Potato Pancakes as a delicious side dish or a snack. They're a classic comfort food that captures the essence of Polish cuisine.

## Rosół (Chicken Broth)

Ingredients:

- 1 whole chicken (about 3-4 pounds), cleaned
- 1 onion, peeled and halved
- 2 carrots, peeled and chopped into chunks
- 2 celery stalks, chopped into chunks
- 1 leek, cleaned and chopped into chunks
- 1 parsnip, peeled and chopped into chunks (optional)
- 1 parsley root (optional)
- 1 small bunch of fresh dill
- 5-6 whole black peppercorns
- Salt, to taste
- 1-2 cloves of garlic (optional)
- Fine egg noodles or cooked rice (optional, for serving)

Instructions:

Rinse the chicken under cold water and place it in a large soup pot.
Fill the pot with enough cold water to cover the chicken by a few inches.
Add the halved onion, carrots, celery, leek, parsnip (if using), parsley root (if using), and the bunch of fresh dill to the pot.
Add the black peppercorns and a pinch of salt to the pot.
Bring the water to a boil over medium-high heat. As soon as it starts boiling, reduce the heat to low and simmer gently.
Skim off any foam or impurities that rise to the surface of the broth during the first 20-30 minutes of cooking.
Allow the broth to simmer for at least 1.5 to 2 hours, ensuring that the chicken is fully cooked and the flavors have melded. You can simmer it longer for a richer flavor.
Taste the broth and adjust the seasoning with additional salt if needed.
Optional: In the last 10-15 minutes of cooking, you can add crushed garlic for additional flavor.
Strain the broth through a fine mesh sieve or cheesecloth into another pot or bowl, discarding the solids. You should be left with a clear, golden broth.
Remove the chicken from the bones and shred the meat. You can add the shredded chicken back into the broth if you like.
If desired, serve the Rosół over fine egg noodles or cooked rice.
Garnish with fresh dill before serving.

Enjoy Rosół as a comforting soup on its own or as a base for other Polish soups and dishes. It's a classic recipe that brings warmth and nourishment to the table.

**Kotlet Schabowy (Pork Cutlet)**

Ingredients:

- 4 pork loin chops, boneless and about 1/2-inch thick
- Salt and pepper, to taste
- 1 cup all-purpose flour
- 2 large eggs, beaten
- 2 cups breadcrumbs (preferably fine)
- Vegetable oil, for frying
- Lemon wedges, for serving

Instructions:

Preheat the oven to a low temperature (around 200°F) to keep the cooked cutlets warm while preparing the others.

Season the pork chops with salt and pepper on both sides.

Set up a breading station with three shallow dishes: one with flour, one with beaten eggs, and one with breadcrumbs.

Dredge each pork chop in the flour, shaking off excess.

Dip the floured pork chop into the beaten eggs, ensuring it is well-coated.

Finally, coat the pork chop with breadcrumbs, pressing the crumbs onto the meat to adhere.

Heat vegetable oil in a large skillet over medium-high heat. You'll need enough oil to cover about halfway up the pork chop when frying.

Carefully place the breaded pork chops in the hot oil, avoiding overcrowding the pan. Fry each side until golden brown, which should take about 4-5 minutes per side.

Once the cutlets are golden and cooked through, transfer them to a plate lined with paper towels to absorb excess oil.

Keep the cooked cutlets warm in the preheated oven while you fry the remaining ones.

Serve Kotlet Schabowy hot, garnished with lemon wedges on the side.

Enjoy Kotlet Schabowy as a main course, typically served with mashed potatoes, a simple salad, or your favorite side dishes. It's a comforting and satisfying dish that showcases the deliciousness of breaded and fried pork cutlets.

**Zrazy (Beef Rolls)**

Ingredients:

*For the Beef Rolls:*

- 1.5 to 2 pounds beef sirloin or round steak, thinly sliced
- Salt and pepper, to taste
- Dijon mustard (optional, for spreading)
- 2 tablespoons vegetable oil, for searing

*For the Filling:*

- 1 large onion, finely chopped
- 2 cloves garlic, minced
- 1 cup mushrooms, finely chopped
- 2 tablespoons butter
- 1/2 cup breadcrumbs
- 1/2 cup beef or vegetable broth
- Salt and pepper, to taste
- Fresh parsley, chopped (for garnish)

*For the Sauce:*

- 1 cup beef or vegetable broth
- 2 tablespoons flour
- 2 tablespoons sour cream
- Salt and pepper, to taste

Instructions:

*Prepare the Filling:*

In a skillet, melt the butter over medium heat. Add the chopped onions, garlic, and mushrooms. Sauté until the vegetables are softened.
Stir in the breadcrumbs and cook for an additional 2-3 minutes.
Add the beef or vegetable broth to the skillet and cook until the mixture thickens.
Season with salt and pepper to taste. Remove from heat and let the filling cool.

*Prepare the Beef Rolls:*

Place the thinly sliced beef between two sheets of plastic wrap. Using a meat mallet, pound the beef slices to flatten them evenly.

Season the beef slices with salt and pepper. If desired, spread a thin layer of Dijon mustard on each slice.

Spoon the cooled filling onto each beef slice and roll them up tightly, securing with toothpicks if needed.

In a large skillet, heat vegetable oil over medium-high heat. Sear the beef rolls on all sides until browned.

Once browned, remove the beef rolls from the skillet and set aside.

*Prepare the Sauce:*

In the same skillet, whisk together flour and beef or vegetable broth over medium heat to create a roux.

Stir in sour cream and continue cooking until the sauce thickens. Season with salt and pepper to taste.

*Finish the Dish:*

Place the seared beef rolls back into the skillet with the sauce.

Simmer the beef rolls in the sauce for about 15-20 minutes, allowing the flavors to meld.

Garnish with chopped fresh parsley before serving.

Serve Zrazy hot, accompanied by your favorite side dishes such as mashed potatoes or noodles. This dish is a savory delight that showcases the richness of Polish cuisine.

**Barszcz (Beet Soup)**

Ingredients:

*For the Broth:*

- 4 medium-sized beets, peeled and grated
- 1 onion, finely chopped
- 2 carrots, peeled and grated
- 2 celery stalks, chopped
- 1 leek, cleaned and chopped
- 1 parsnip, peeled and chopped
- 1 bay leaf
- 8 cups vegetable or chicken broth
- Salt and pepper, to taste
- 1-2 tablespoons sugar (optional, to balance acidity)

*For the Czernina (Optional):*

- 1/2 cup dried forest mushrooms (such as porcini)
- 1 cup water

*For the Garnish:*

- Sour cream
- Fresh dill, chopped
- Hard-boiled eggs, sliced

Instructions:

In a large pot, combine grated beets, chopped onion, grated carrots, chopped celery, chopped leek, chopped parsnip, and the bay leaf.

Pour the vegetable or chicken broth into the pot, ensuring it covers the ingredients.

If you're including Czernina (optional), place the dried forest mushrooms in a bowl and cover with 1 cup of water. Let them soak for about 30 minutes. Strain the liquid and add it to the pot.

Bring the mixture to a boil, then reduce the heat and simmer for about 45 minutes to 1 hour, or until the beets are tender.

Season the soup with salt and pepper. Optionally, add sugar to balance the acidity.
If you want a clearer broth, you can strain the soup to remove the solids. However, many prefer to leave the grated vegetables for a heartier texture.
Serve the Barszcz hot, garnished with a dollop of sour cream, chopped fresh dill, and slices of hard-boiled eggs.

Barszcz can be served on its own or with traditional Polish dumplings called Uszka. Enjoy this vibrant and comforting Beet Soup as a centerpiece of your Polish culinary experience.

# Polish Soups:

## Kapuśniak (Cabbage Soup)

Ingredients:

- 1 medium head of cabbage, shredded
- 1 large onion, finely chopped
- 2 carrots, peeled and sliced
- 2 potatoes, peeled and diced
- 1 parsnip, peeled and diced
- 1 leek, cleaned and chopped
- 2 cloves garlic, minced
- 1 can (14 oz) diced tomatoes
- 1/2 cup tomato paste
- 1 pound kielbasa or Polish sausage, sliced
- 8 cups vegetable or chicken broth
- 2 bay leaves
- 1 teaspoon caraway seeds
- Salt and pepper, to taste
- Fresh dill, chopped (for garnish)
- Sour cream (optional, for serving)

Instructions:

In a large soup pot, heat a bit of oil over medium heat. Add the chopped onions and minced garlic, and sauté until the onions are translucent.

Add the shredded cabbage, sliced carrots, diced potatoes, diced parsnip, and chopped leek to the pot. Stir and cook for a few minutes until the vegetables start to soften.

Pour in the vegetable or chicken broth, add the diced tomatoes, tomato paste, bay leaves, and caraway seeds. Bring the soup to a boil.

Reduce the heat to a simmer and add the sliced kielbasa or Polish sausage to the pot. Allow the soup to simmer for about 20-30 minutes, or until the vegetables are tender.

Season the soup with salt and pepper to taste. Adjust the seasoning as needed. Remove the bay leaves before serving.

Ladle the Kapuśniak into bowls and garnish with chopped fresh dill. Optionally, serve with a dollop of sour cream on top.

Kapuśniak is a comforting and filling soup that captures the essence of Polish cuisine. Enjoy it on its own or with a slice of crusty bread for a wholesome meal.

**Zupa Grzybowa (Mushroom Soup)**

Ingredients:

- 1 pound mixed mushrooms (such as cremini, white button, or wild mushrooms), cleaned and sliced
- 1 large onion, finely chopped
- 2 carrots, peeled and grated
- 2 celery stalks, chopped
- 2 cloves garlic, minced
- 1/4 cup unsalted butter
- 1/4 cup all-purpose flour
- 8 cups vegetable or mushroom broth
- 1 bay leaf
- 1 teaspoon dried marjoram
- Salt and pepper, to taste
- 1/2 cup sour cream
- Fresh parsley, chopped (for garnish)

Instructions:

In a large pot, melt the butter over medium heat. Add the chopped onion, grated carrots, chopped celery, and minced garlic. Sauté until the vegetables are softened.
Add the sliced mushrooms to the pot and cook until they release their moisture and become tender.
Sprinkle the flour over the mushroom mixture and stir well to combine. Cook for an additional 2-3 minutes to remove the raw taste of the flour.
Pour in the vegetable or mushroom broth, stirring constantly to avoid lumps. Add the bay leaf and dried marjoram.
Bring the soup to a simmer and let it cook for about 20-25 minutes, allowing the flavors to meld.
Season the soup with salt and pepper to taste.
Remove the bay leaf from the soup.
Just before serving, stir in the sour cream to add richness to the soup. Adjust the seasoning if necessary.
Ladle the Zupa Grzybowa into bowls and garnish with chopped fresh parsley.

Serve this Mushroom Soup hot as a comforting appetizer or as a light main course. It's a delightful way to savor the earthy goodness of mushrooms in a bowl.

**Zupa Ogórkowa (Cucumber Soup)**

Ingredients:

- 4 medium-sized pickled cucumbers (gherkins), grated
- 1 large onion, finely chopped
- 2 carrots, peeled and grated
- 2 potatoes, peeled and diced
- 1 leek, cleaned and chopped
- 2 cloves garlic, minced
- 1/4 cup unsalted butter
- 8 cups vegetable or chicken broth
- 1 bay leaf
- 1 teaspoon dried marjoram
- Salt and pepper, to taste
- 1 cup sour cream
- Fresh dill, chopped (for garnish)

Instructions:

In a large pot, melt the butter over medium heat. Add the chopped onion, grated carrots, chopped leek, and minced garlic. Sauté until the vegetables are softened.
Add the diced potatoes to the pot and continue to cook for a few minutes.
Pour in the vegetable or chicken broth, and add the bay leaf and dried marjoram. Bring the soup to a simmer and let it cook for about 15-20 minutes, or until the potatoes are tender.
Add the grated pickled cucumbers to the pot and simmer for an additional 10 minutes.
Season the soup with salt and pepper to taste.
Remove the bay leaf from the soup.
Just before serving, stir in the sour cream to add creaminess and a tangy flavor.
Adjust the seasoning if necessary.
Ladle the Zupa Ogórkowa into bowls and garnish with chopped fresh dill.

Serve this Cucumber Soup hot or cold, depending on your preference. It's a unique and delicious way to enjoy the bright flavors of pickled cucumbers in a comforting soup.

**Zupa Pomidorowa (Tomato Soup)**

Ingredients:

- 2 tablespoons butter or vegetable oil
- 1 large onion, finely chopped
- 2 carrots, peeled and diced
- 2 celery stalks, diced
- 2 cloves garlic, minced
- 1 can (28 oz) crushed tomatoes
- 4 cups vegetable or chicken broth
- 1 bay leaf
- 1 teaspoon dried basil
- 1 teaspoon dried oregano
- 1/2 teaspoon sugar
- Salt and pepper, to taste
- 1/2 cup heavy cream (optional)
- Fresh basil, chopped (for garnish)
- Croutons or bread (for serving)

Instructions:

In a large pot, heat the butter or vegetable oil over medium heat. Add the chopped onion, diced carrots, and diced celery. Sauté until the vegetables are softened.
Add the minced garlic to the pot and cook for an additional minute until fragrant.
Pour in the crushed tomatoes and vegetable or chicken broth. Stir well to combine.
Add the bay leaf, dried basil, dried oregano, sugar, salt, and pepper to the pot. Bring the soup to a simmer.
Reduce the heat to low and let the soup simmer for about 20-25 minutes to allow the flavors to meld.
Remove the bay leaf from the soup.
Using an immersion blender or a regular blender, puree the soup until smooth. Be cautious when blending hot liquids and work in batches if using a traditional blender.
Return the soup to the pot and stir in the heavy cream, if using. Simmer for an additional 5 minutes.
Adjust the seasoning if necessary.

Ladle the Zupa Pomidorowa into bowls and garnish with chopped fresh basil. Serve the tomato soup hot, accompanied by croutons or a slice of bread.

Zupa Pomidorowa is a classic and satisfying soup that is perfect for warming up on chilly days. Enjoy its rich tomato flavor and creamy texture!

**Grochówka (Pea Soup)**

Ingredients:

- 2 cups dried green peas, soaked overnight
- 1 large onion, finely chopped
- 2 carrots, peeled and diced
- 2 potatoes, peeled and diced
- 2 cloves garlic, minced
- 1 bay leaf
- 1 teaspoon dried marjoram
- 1 teaspoon dried thyme
- 1 teaspoon smoked paprika
- 1 tablespoon vegetable oil
- 8 cups vegetable or chicken broth
- Salt and pepper, to taste
- Kielbasa (Polish sausage), sliced (optional)
- Fresh parsley, chopped (for garnish)
- Sour cream (optional, for serving)

Instructions:

In a large pot, heat the vegetable oil over medium heat. Add the chopped onion and sauté until it becomes translucent.
Drain the soaked peas and add them to the pot. Stir well to combine.
Pour in the vegetable or chicken broth, ensuring that the peas are fully covered.
Add the diced carrots, diced potatoes, minced garlic, bay leaf, dried marjoram, dried thyme, and smoked paprika to the pot. Stir the ingredients.
Bring the soup to a boil, then reduce the heat to low and simmer for about 1.5 to 2 hours, or until the peas are soft and the soup has thickened.
If using kielbasa, add the sliced sausage to the soup during the last 15-20 minutes of cooking, allowing it to heat through.
Season the soup with salt and pepper to taste.
Remove the bay leaf before serving.
Ladle the Grochówka into bowls and garnish with chopped fresh parsley.
Optionally, serve the pea soup with a dollop of sour cream on top.

Enjoy this comforting and nourishing Grochówka on its own or with a slice of crusty bread. It's a wholesome dish that captures the essence of Polish home cooking.

## Krem z Kalafiora (Cream of Cauliflower Soup)

Ingredients:

- 1 large cauliflower, cleaned and cut into florets
- 1 onion, finely chopped
- 2 cloves garlic, minced
- 2 tablespoons butter or olive oil
- 4 cups vegetable or chicken broth
- 1 bay leaf
- 1 teaspoon dried thyme
- Salt and pepper, to taste
- 1 cup heavy cream
- Fresh chives or parsley, chopped (for garnish)

Instructions:

In a large pot, melt the butter or heat the olive oil over medium heat. Add the chopped onion and minced garlic, and sauté until the onion becomes translucent. Add the cauliflower florets to the pot and cook for a few minutes, stirring to coat them in the onion and garlic mixture.

Pour in the vegetable or chicken broth, ensuring that the cauliflower is fully covered. Add the bay leaf and dried thyme.

Bring the soup to a boil, then reduce the heat to low and simmer for about 15-20 minutes, or until the cauliflower is tender.

Remove the bay leaf from the pot.

Use an immersion blender to puree the soup until smooth. Alternatively, transfer the soup in batches to a blender, blend until smooth, and return it to the pot.

Stir in the heavy cream and heat the soup through, but do not boil.

Season the soup with salt and pepper to taste.

Ladle the Cream of Cauliflower Soup into bowls and garnish with chopped fresh chives or parsley.

Serve the soup hot, accompanied by crusty bread or croutons if desired.

Enjoy this rich and velvety Krem z Kalafiora for a comforting and satisfying meal. It's a perfect choice for a cozy lunch or dinner during colder days.

**Chłodnik (Cold Beet Soup)**

Ingredients:

- 4 medium-sized beets, cooked, peeled, and grated
- 2 cups plain yogurt
- 1 cucumber, peeled and diced
- 3 hard-boiled eggs, chopped
- 1 bunch fresh dill, chopped
- 1 bunch fresh scallions, chopped
- 4 cups buttermilk
- 2 cups water
- Juice of 1-2 lemons (adjust to taste)
- Salt and sugar, to taste
- Radishes, sliced (for garnish)
- Fresh mint leaves (for garnish)

Instructions:

In a large mixing bowl, combine the grated beets, diced cucumber, chopped hard-boiled eggs, chopped dill, and chopped scallions.

Add the plain yogurt, buttermilk, and water to the bowl. Stir well to combine.

Season the soup with salt, sugar, and lemon juice to taste. The sugar helps balance the natural acidity of the beets.

Refrigerate the soup for at least 2-3 hours to allow the flavors to meld and to chill the soup thoroughly.

Before serving, check the seasoning and adjust if needed.

Ladle the Chłodnik into bowls and garnish with sliced radishes and fresh mint leaves.

Serve the cold beet soup as a refreshing appetizer or light meal, especially on a warm day.

Chłodnik is not only delicious but also a visually striking dish with its vibrant pink color. It's a perfect addition to your summer menu, offering a unique and cooling experience with the combination of beets, yogurt, and fresh herbs.

## Zupa Kalafiorowa (Cauliflower Soup)

Ingredients:

- 1 large cauliflower, cleaned and cut into florets
- 1 onion, finely chopped
- 2 cloves garlic, minced
- 2 tablespoons butter or olive oil
- 4 cups vegetable or chicken broth
- 1 bay leaf
- 1 teaspoon dried thyme
- Salt and pepper, to taste
- 1 cup milk or cream
- Fresh chives or parsley, chopped (for garnish)

Instructions:

In a large pot, melt the butter or heat the olive oil over medium heat. Add the chopped onion and minced garlic, and sauté until the onion becomes translucent. Add the cauliflower florets to the pot and cook for a few minutes, stirring to coat them in the onion and garlic mixture.
Pour in the vegetable or chicken broth, ensuring that the cauliflower is fully covered. Add the bay leaf and dried thyme.
Bring the soup to a boil, then reduce the heat to low and simmer for about 15-20 minutes, or until the cauliflower is tender.
Remove the bay leaf from the pot.
Use an immersion blender to puree the soup until smooth. Alternatively, transfer the soup in batches to a blender, blend until smooth, and return it to the pot.
Stir in the milk or cream and heat the soup through, but do not boil.
Season the soup with salt and pepper to taste.
Ladle the Zupa Kalafiorowa into bowls and garnish with chopped fresh chives or parsley.
Serve the soup hot, accompanied by crusty bread or croutons if desired.

Enjoy this creamy and comforting Cauliflower Soup for a satisfying and wholesome meal. It's a perfect choice for a cozy lunch or dinner, especially during colder days.

**Zupa Buraczkowa (Beetroot Soup)**

Ingredients:

- 4 medium-sized beets, peeled and grated
- 1 large onion, finely chopped
- 2 carrots, peeled and grated
- 2 potatoes, peeled and diced
- 1 leek, cleaned and chopped
- 2 cloves garlic, minced
- 1 bay leaf
- 8 cups vegetable or chicken broth
- Salt and pepper, to taste
- 2 tablespoons olive oil
- 2 tablespoons red wine vinegar
- 1 tablespoon sugar (optional, to balance acidity)
- Sour cream (for serving)
- Fresh dill, chopped (for garnish)

Instructions:

In a large pot, heat the olive oil over medium heat. Add the chopped onion and sauté until it becomes translucent.
Add the grated beets, grated carrots, diced potatoes, chopped leek, and minced garlic to the pot. Stir well to combine.
Pour in the vegetable or chicken broth, ensuring that the vegetables are fully covered. Add the bay leaf.
Bring the soup to a boil, then reduce the heat to low and simmer for about 30-40 minutes, or until the vegetables are tender.
Season the soup with salt and pepper to taste. Add the red wine vinegar and sugar if using, adjusting to achieve the desired balance of flavors.
Remove the bay leaf from the pot.
Allow the soup to cool slightly before serving.
Ladle the Zupa Buraczkowa into bowls. Optionally, serve each portion with a dollop of sour cream on top and a sprinkle of fresh chopped dill.
Enjoy this vibrant and flavorful Beetroot Soup as a comforting appetizer or light meal.

Zupa Buraczkowa is often served hot, but it can also be enjoyed chilled, especially during the warmer months. The combination of beets, vegetables, and a touch of acidity creates a unique and satisfying soup.

**Zupa Serowa (Cheese Soup)**

Ingredients:

- 1/4 cup unsalted butter
- 1 onion, finely chopped
- 2 carrots, peeled and grated
- 2 celery stalks, chopped
- 2 potatoes, peeled and diced
- 1 leek, cleaned and chopped
- 1/4 cup all-purpose flour
- 4 cups vegetable or chicken broth
- 2 cups milk
- 2 cups shredded cheddar cheese
- 1 cup shredded Gouda or Emmental cheese
- Salt and pepper, to taste
- 1/2 teaspoon ground nutmeg
- Fresh chives, chopped (for garnish)
- Croutons (for serving, optional)

Instructions:

In a large pot, melt the butter over medium heat. Add the chopped onion, grated carrots, chopped celery, and chopped leek. Sauté until the vegetables are softened.
Add the diced potatoes to the pot and continue to cook for a few minutes.
Sprinkle the flour over the vegetable mixture and stir well to coat the vegetables.
Gradually add the vegetable or chicken broth, stirring constantly to avoid lumps.
Pour in the milk and bring the soup to a simmer. Cook until the potatoes are tender.
Reduce the heat to low, and gradually stir in the shredded cheddar and Gouda or Emmental cheese until melted and smooth.
Season the soup with salt, pepper, and ground nutmeg to taste.
Continue to simmer the soup on low heat, stirring occasionally, for about 10-15 minutes to allow the flavors to meld.
Remove the soup from heat.
Ladle the Zupa Serowa into bowls and garnish with chopped fresh chives.
Optionally, serve the cheese soup with croutons for added texture.

Enjoy this creamy and cheesy Polish Cheese Soup as a comforting and flavorful dish. It's a perfect choice for cheese lovers and makes for a satisfying meal during cooler weather.

# Polish Appetizers:

**Paszteciki (Puff Pastry with Fillings)**

Ingredients:

*For the Dough:*

- 2 sheets of puff pastry, thawed if frozen
- Flour for dusting

*For the Filling:*

- 1 cup mushrooms, finely chopped
- 1 onion, finely chopped
- 1/2 pound ground meat (beef or pork)
- 2 tablespoons butter
- Salt and pepper, to taste
- 1 teaspoon dried marjoram
- 1/2 cup beef or vegetable broth
- 2 tablespoons all-purpose flour

*For Assembly:*

- 1 egg, beaten (for egg wash)
- Sesame seeds or poppy seeds (optional, for sprinkling)

Instructions:

   Prepare the Filling:
   - In a pan, melt the butter over medium heat. Add the chopped onions and sauté until translucent.
   - Add the chopped mushrooms and cook until the moisture evaporates.
   - Add the ground meat to the pan and cook until browned.
   - Season the mixture with salt, pepper, and dried marjoram.
   - In a small bowl, mix the flour with beef or vegetable broth to create a thickening agent. Add it to the meat mixture, stirring until well combined. Cook for a few more minutes until the filling thickens. Remove from heat and let it cool.

Prepare the Dough:
- Preheat the oven to the temperature specified on the puff pastry package.
- On a lightly floured surface, roll out the puff pastry sheets to flatten slightly.

Assemble the Paszteciki:
- Cut each sheet into squares or rectangles, depending on your preference.
- Place a spoonful of the cooled mushroom and meat filling in the center of each piece of pastry.

Seal and Bake:
- Fold the pastry over the filling to form a triangle or rectangle. Press the edges firmly to seal.
- Brush the tops of the Paszteciki with beaten egg and, if desired, sprinkle with sesame seeds or poppy seeds.
- Place the filled pastries on a baking sheet lined with parchment paper.

Bake:
- Bake in the preheated oven according to the puff pastry package instructions or until the Paszteciki are golden brown and puffed.

Serve:
- Allow the Paszteciki to cool slightly before serving.
- Enjoy these savory puff pastry delights either warm or at room temperature.

Feel free to experiment with other fillings such as sauerkraut and mushrooms, cheese and spinach, or sweet options like fruit preserves for a delicious twist on Paszteciki.

## Rolmopsy (Herring Rolls)

Ingredients:

*For the Herring Rolls:*

- 8-10 pickled herring fillets
- 1 cup creamed herring or sour cream herring
- 1 small onion, finely chopped
- 2 hard-boiled eggs, finely chopped
- 2 tablespoons Dijon mustard
- 2 tablespoons mayonnaise
- Freshly ground black pepper, to taste

*For the Garnish:*

- Chopped fresh dill
- Capers (optional)
- Lemon wedges

Instructions:

Prepare the Filling:
- In a bowl, combine the creamed herring, chopped onion, chopped hard-boiled eggs, Dijon mustard, mayonnaise, and freshly ground black pepper. Mix well until all ingredients are incorporated.

Assemble the Herring Rolls:
- Lay each pickled herring fillet flat on a clean surface.
- Spoon a small amount of the filling onto each herring fillet.
- Roll the herring fillet around the filling, forming a neat roll. Secure with toothpicks if needed.

Chill:
- Place the Rolmopsy in the refrigerator to chill for at least 1-2 hours. This allows the flavors to meld and the rolls to set.

Serve:
- Arrange the Rolmopsy on a serving platter.
- Garnish with chopped fresh dill and capers if desired.

- Serve with lemon wedges on the side.

Enjoy:
- Rolmopsy can be enjoyed as an appetizer, side dish, or part of a traditional Polish spread.

This dish is a favorite during holidays and celebrations in Poland. The combination of pickled herring and a flavorful filling creates a delicious and unique appetizer.

**Śledź w Oleju (Herring in Oil)**

Ingredients:

- 4-6 pickled herring fillets (matjes or other preferred variety)
- 1 small onion, thinly sliced
- 1 carrot, peeled and thinly sliced (optional)
- 2 bay leaves
- 5-6 whole peppercorns
- 1 teaspoon mustard seeds
- 1 teaspoon sugar
- 1 cup vegetable oil
- 1/2 cup white wine vinegar
- Fresh dill, chopped (for garnish)
- Lemon wedges (for serving)

Instructions:

Prepare the Herring:
- If the herring fillets are salted or in brine, rinse them under cold water and pat them dry with paper towels.
- Cut the herring fillets into bite-sized pieces.

Prepare the Marinade:
- In a bowl, whisk together the vegetable oil, white wine vinegar, sugar, mustard seeds, whole peppercorns, and bay leaves.

Assemble the Dish:
- In a clean and sterile glass jar or airtight container, layer the herring pieces, sliced onions, and optional sliced carrots.
- Pour the marinade mixture over the herring, making sure it covers the fish completely.

Marinate:
- Seal the jar or container and refrigerate the herring for at least 24 hours to allow the flavors to develop. The longer it marinates, the more flavorful it becomes.

Serve:
- Before serving, let the herring come to room temperature for about 15-20 minutes.
- Garnish with chopped fresh dill.
- Serve the Herring in Oil with lemon wedges on the side.

Enjoy:
- This dish is typically served as an appetizer, often accompanied by fresh bread, crackers, or as part of a Polish herring platter.

Herring in Oil is a tasty and traditional Polish dish that showcases the beloved flavors of pickled herring in a delicious marinade. It's a great addition to festive occasions and gatherings.

## Kabanosy (Thin Smoked Sausages)

Ingredients:

- 2 pounds pork shoulder, finely ground
- 1/2 pound pork fatback, finely ground
- 2 teaspoons salt
- 1 teaspoon black pepper
- 1 teaspoon sugar
- 1 teaspoon garlic powder
- 1 teaspoon dried marjoram
- 1/2 teaspoon curing salt (optional, for color and preservation)
- 1/4 cup ice water
- Natural hog casings

Instructions:

Prepare Casings:
- Soak the hog casings in warm water for about 30 minutes to soften them. Rinse them thoroughly to remove excess salt.

Prepare Meat Mixture:
- In a large mixing bowl, combine the finely ground pork shoulder, pork fatback, salt, black pepper, sugar, garlic powder, marjoram, and curing salt (if using). Mix well.

Grind Meat:
- Pass the meat mixture through a meat grinder fitted with a fine grinding plate.

Mix and Chill:
- Transfer the ground meat to a bowl, add ice water, and mix thoroughly to create a sticky texture. Place the mixture in the refrigerator for about 1 hour to chill.

Stuff Casings:
- Rinse the hog casings again and soak them in warm water for an additional 10-15 minutes.
- Attach the sausage stuffing tube to the grinder. Stuff the casings with the chilled meat mixture, making long, thin sausages.

Twist and Dry:
- Twist the sausages into desired lengths (typically 6-8 inches) and hang them to air-dry for about 1-2 hours.

Smoke:
- Preheat your smoker to a low temperature (around 160-180°F or 71-82°C).
- Smoke the Kabanosy for 2-3 hours, or until they develop a rich smoky flavor and a golden-brown color.

Finish in Oven (Optional):
- If a smoker is not available, you can finish cooking the sausages in a preheated oven at 180°F (82°C) until they reach an internal temperature of 155°F (68°C).

Cool and Store:
- Allow the Kabanosy to cool before storing them in the refrigerator or a cool, dry place.

Enjoy your homemade Kabanosy as a tasty and authentic Polish snack or appetizer!

## Sałatka Jarzynowa (Polish Vegetable Salad)

Ingredients:

- 4 medium potatoes, boiled and diced
- 3 carrots, boiled and diced
- 1 cup frozen peas, cooked
- 4 hard-boiled eggs, chopped
- 1 large apple, peeled and diced
- 1 cup cooked and diced ham or cooked chicken (optional)
- 1/2 cup dill pickles, diced
- 1 small red onion, finely chopped
- 1 cup mayonnaise
- 2 tablespoons Dijon mustard
- Salt and pepper, to taste
- Fresh dill, chopped (for garnish)

Instructions:

Prepare the Vegetables:
- Boil the potatoes and carrots until tender. Allow them to cool, then peel and dice them.

Cook the Peas:
- Cook the frozen peas according to the package instructions. Drain and let them cool.

Hard-Boil the Eggs:
- Hard-boil the eggs, cool them under cold water, peel, and chop.

Assemble the Salad:
- In a large mixing bowl, combine the diced potatoes, carrots, peas, chopped eggs, diced apple, and any optional ingredients like ham or chicken.

Add Pickles and Onion:
- Add the diced dill pickles and finely chopped red onion to the bowl.

Prepare the Dressing:
- In a separate bowl, mix together mayonnaise and Dijon mustard to create the dressing.

Combine and Season:
- Pour the dressing over the vegetables and toss gently to coat evenly.
- Season the salad with salt and pepper to taste.

Chill:
- Cover the salad and refrigerate for at least a couple of hours before serving to allow the flavors to meld.

Garnish:
- Before serving, garnish the Sałatka Jarzynowa with chopped fresh dill.

Serve:
- Serve the Polish Vegetable Salad as a side dish or as part of a festive spread.

Sałatka Jarzynowa is known for its hearty and flavorful combination of vegetables, making it a beloved dish in Polish households. It's a versatile recipe, and you can adjust the ingredients based on personal preferences.

**Jajka Faszerowane (Stuffed Eggs)**

Ingredients:

- 6 hard-boiled eggs
- 3 tablespoons mayonnaise
- 1 teaspoon Dijon mustard
- 1 teaspoon white vinegar
- Salt and pepper, to taste
- Paprika, for garnish (optional)
- Fresh chives or parsley, chopped, for garnish

Optional Variations for Filling:

- Finely chopped cooked ham or bacon
- Sweet relish or pickles, finely chopped
- Smoked salmon, finely chopped
- Shredded cheese

Instructions:

Hard-Boil the Eggs:
- Place the eggs in a saucepan and cover them with water.
- Bring the water to a boil, then reduce the heat and simmer for about 10 minutes.
- Remove the eggs from heat and let them cool. Peel the eggs once they are cool enough to handle.

Cut and Scoop:
- Cut the hard-boiled eggs in half lengthwise.
- Gently scoop out the yolks and place them in a bowl.

Prepare the Filling:
- Mash the egg yolks with a fork.
- Add mayonnaise, Dijon mustard, white vinegar, salt, and pepper to the mashed yolks. Mix until well combined.

Optional Add-Ins:
- If desired, mix in any optional add-ins like chopped ham, bacon, sweet relish, pickles, smoked salmon, or shredded cheese.

Fill the Egg Whites:
- Spoon or pipe the yolk mixture back into the hollowed-out egg whites.

- You can use a pastry bag for a neater presentation or simply use a spoon.

Garnish:
- Garnish each stuffed egg with a sprinkle of paprika (if desired) and chopped fresh chives or parsley.

Chill:
- Refrigerate the stuffed eggs for at least 30 minutes before serving to allow the flavors to meld.

Serve:
- Arrange the Jajka Faszerowane on a serving platter and serve as a delightful appetizer.

Stuffed eggs are a versatile dish, and you can get creative with the filling variations to suit your taste. They make an elegant and tasty addition to any party or gathering.

# Placki Ziemniaczane z Łososiem (Potato Pancakes with Salmon)

Ingredients:

*For Potato Pancakes:*

- 4 large potatoes, peeled and grated
- 1 onion, finely grated
- 2 eggs, beaten
- 3 tablespoons all-purpose flour
- Salt and pepper, to taste
- Vegetable oil, for frying

*For Salmon Topping:*

- Smoked salmon slices
- Cream cheese or sour cream
- Fresh dill, chopped
- Lemon wedges

Instructions:

Prepare Potato Pancakes:
- Grate the peeled potatoes and onion using a box grater or a food processor.
- Place the grated potatoes and onion in a clean kitchen towel and squeeze out the excess moisture.
- In a large bowl, combine the grated potatoes, grated onion, beaten eggs, flour, salt, and pepper. Mix well.

Fry the Pancakes:
- Heat vegetable oil in a skillet over medium-high heat.
- Scoop a portion of the potato mixture and form it into a pancake shape. Place it in the hot oil and flatten it with a spatula.
- Fry each side until golden brown and crispy. Remove from the skillet and place on paper towels to absorb excess oil. Repeat until all pancakes are cooked.

Prepare Salmon Topping:
- Place a slice of smoked salmon on top of each potato pancake.

Serve:

- Garnish the salmon-topped potato pancakes with a dollop of cream cheese or sour cream.
- Sprinkle chopped fresh dill over the top.
- Serve the Potato Pancakes with Salmon with lemon wedges on the side.

Enjoy:

- These delicious potato pancakes with smoked salmon make a fantastic appetizer or brunch dish. The combination of crispy potatoes and the savory flavor of salmon is sure to be a hit.

Feel free to customize the toppings based on your preferences. You can also add capers, red onion slices, or other herbs for added flavor.

## Tatar (Beef Tartare)

Ingredients:

- 1/2 pound high-quality beef fillet, finely chopped or minced
- 1 small onion, finely chopped
- 2 tablespoons capers, drained and finely chopped
- 2 tablespoons Dijon mustard
- 2 tablespoons Worcestershire sauce
- 1 tablespoon ketchup
- 2 tablespoons olive oil
- Salt and pepper, to taste
- Chopped fresh parsley, for garnish
- Optional: Tabasco sauce or hot sauce for added heat
- Optional: Egg yolk for serving

Instructions:

Prepare the Beef:
- Ensure the beef fillet is very fresh and high-quality.
- Finely chop or mince the beef into small, uniform pieces. Some prefer a coarser texture, while others prefer it very fine. You can use a sharp knife or a meat grinder.

Chop Onion and Capers:
- Finely chop the onion and capers. If you prefer a milder onion flavor, you can soak the chopped onion in cold water for a few minutes and then drain.

Make the Tartare Mixture:
- In a mixing bowl, combine the finely chopped beef, chopped onion, chopped capers, Dijon mustard, Worcestershire sauce, ketchup, and olive oil.
- Mix the ingredients well until evenly combined.

Season and Adjust:
- Season the tartare mixture with salt and pepper to taste.
- If you like it spicy, you can add a few drops of Tabasco sauce or your favorite hot sauce.

Serve:
- Form the beef tartare into a mound on individual plates or shape it using a ring mold.

- Optionally, create a small well in the center of each serving and place an egg yolk in it.

Garnish:
- Garnish the beef tartare with chopped fresh parsley.

Serve with Accompaniments:
- Beef tartare is often served with bread, toast points, or fries on the side.

Enjoy:
- Enjoy the Beef Tartare immediately after preparing for the best freshness.

Note: Consuming raw or undercooked meat poses a risk of foodborne illness. Ensure that you use high-quality, fresh meat from a trusted source and take necessary precautions.

Beef Tartare is a dish appreciated for its simplicity and rich flavors. It's often considered a delicacy and is best enjoyed when using the freshest and highest-quality ingredients.

**Zakąski (Appetizer Platter)**

Components for Zakąski Platter:

Cold Cuts and Cheeses:
- Assortment of cold cuts such as kielbasa, salami, and ham.
- Various cheeses, including smoked cheese, brie, or traditional Polish cheeses.

Herring Preparations:
- Rolmopsy (Herring Rolls): Herring fillets rolled with a savory filling.
- Śledź w Oleju (Herring in Oil): Pickled herring in an oil-based marinade.

Dips and Spreads:
- Tatar (Beef Tartare): Finely chopped raw beef with seasonings.
- Pasztet (Pâté): Liver or meat pâté, often served with bread or crackers.
- Smalec: Pork fat spread, flavored with onions and spices.

Pickled Vegetables:
- Pickles: Traditional dill pickles or pickled cucumbers.
- Ogórki Kiszone (Fermented Pickles): Fermented cucumbers for a tangy flavor.
- Pickled Mushrooms: Mushrooms marinated in a flavorful brine.

Breads and Crackers:
- Sliced baguette or traditional Polish bread.
- Crackers or grissini for variety.

Fresh Vegetables:
- Radishes: Fresh radishes add a crisp texture.
- Cherry tomatoes or sliced tomatoes.

Condiments:
- Mustard: Dijon or traditional Polish mustard.
- Horseradish: Grated horseradish for a spicy kick.
- Cranberry Sauce: A sweet and tart condiment.

Garnishes:
- Fresh herbs like dill or parsley.
- Lemon wedges for a citrusy touch.

Assembly:

Arrange on Platter:
- Start by placing a variety of cold cuts and cheeses on the platter, creating different sections.

Add Herring Preparations:
- Arrange the Rolmopsy and Śledź w Oleju on the platter.

Place Dips and Spreads:
- Position the Tatar, Pasztet, and Smalec with small serving utensils.

Incorporate Pickled Vegetables:
- Strategically place pickles, fermented cucumbers, and pickled mushrooms.

Arrange Breads and Crackers:
- Position sliced bread, crackers, or grissini near the dips.

Add Fresh Vegetables:
- Scatter radishes and cherry tomatoes for a burst of freshness.

Provide Condiments:
- Set out mustard, horseradish, and cranberry sauce in small bowls.

Garnish and Serve:
- Sprinkle fresh herbs over the platter for a finishing touch.
- Serve the Zakąski platter with lemon wedges on the side.

Zakąski platters offer a delightful variety of flavors and textures, providing a perfect start to a Polish meal or a great accompaniment for social gatherings. Feel free to customize the platter based on personal preferences and the occasion.

**Naleśniki z Serem (Cheese-filled Crepes)**

Components for Zakąski Platter:

Cold Cuts and Cheeses:
- Assortment of cold cuts such as kielbasa, salami, and ham.
- Various cheeses, including smoked cheese, brie, or traditional Polish cheeses.

Herring Preparations:
- Rolmopsy (Herring Rolls): Herring fillets rolled with a savory filling.
- Śledź w Oleju (Herring in Oil): Pickled herring in an oil-based marinade.

Dips and Spreads:
- Tatar (Beef Tartare): Finely chopped raw beef with seasonings.
- Pasztet (Pâté): Liver or meat pâté, often served with bread or crackers.
- Smalec: Pork fat spread, flavored with onions and spices.

Pickled Vegetables:
- Pickles: Traditional dill pickles or pickled cucumbers.
- Ogórki Kiszone (Fermented Pickles): Fermented cucumbers for a tangy flavor.
- Pickled Mushrooms: Mushrooms marinated in a flavorful brine.

Breads and Crackers:
- Sliced baguette or traditional Polish bread.
- Crackers or grissini for variety.

Fresh Vegetables:
- Radishes: Fresh radishes add a crisp texture.
- Cherry tomatoes or sliced tomatoes.

Condiments:
- Mustard: Dijon or traditional Polish mustard.
- Horseradish: Grated horseradish for a spicy kick.
- Cranberry Sauce: A sweet and tart condiment.

Garnishes:
- Fresh herbs like dill or parsley.
- Lemon wedges for a citrusy touch.

Assembly:

Arrange on Platter:

- Start by placing a variety of cold cuts and cheeses on the platter, creating different sections.

Add Herring Preparations:
- Arrange the Rolmopsy and Śledź w Oleju on the platter.

Place Dips and Spreads:
- Position the Tatar, Pasztet, and Smalec with small serving utensils.

Incorporate Pickled Vegetables:
- Strategically place pickles, fermented cucumbers, and pickled mushrooms.

Arrange Breads and Crackers:
- Position sliced bread, crackers, or grissini near the dips.

Add Fresh Vegetables:
- Scatter radishes and cherry tomatoes for a burst of freshness.

Provide Condiments:
- Set out mustard, horseradish, and cranberry sauce in small bowls.

Garnish and Serve:
- Sprinkle fresh herbs over the platter for a finishing touch.
- Serve the Zakąski platter with lemon wedges on the side.

Zakąski platters offer a delightful variety of flavors and textures, providing a perfect start to a Polish meal or a great accompaniment for social gatherings. Feel free to customize the platter based on personal preferences and the occasion.

**Naleśniki z Serem (Cheese-filled Crepes)**

"Naleśniki z Serem," or Cheese-filled Crepes, are a delicious Polish treat that can be enjoyed for breakfast, dessert, or as a sweet snack. Here's a simple recipe to make these delightful cheese-filled crepes:

Ingredients:

*For the Crepes:*

- 1 cup all-purpose flour
- 2 large eggs
- 1 cup milk
- 1/2 cup water
- 2 tablespoons melted butter
- Pinch of salt
- Butter or oil for greasing the pan

*For the Cheese Filling:*

- 1 cup farmer's cheese or cottage cheese
- 2 tablespoons sugar (adjust to taste)
- 1 teaspoon vanilla extract
- Zest of one lemon (optional)
- Raisins or currants (optional)

*For Serving:*

- Powdered sugar
- Fruit preserves or syrup (optional)

Instructions:

> Prepare the Crepe Batter:
> - In a blender, combine the flour, eggs, milk, water, melted butter, and a pinch of salt.

- Blend until the batter is smooth. Let the batter rest for about 30 minutes.

Make the Cheese Filling:
- In a bowl, mix together the farmer's cheese or cottage cheese, sugar, vanilla extract, lemon zest (if using), and raisins or currants (if using). Adjust the sugar to taste.

Cook the Crepes:
- Heat a non-stick skillet or crepe pan over medium heat. Grease it lightly with butter or oil.
- Pour a small amount of the crepe batter into the pan, swirling it to spread the batter thinly and evenly.
- Cook the crepe for about 1-2 minutes until the edges start to lift. Flip the crepe and cook for an additional 1-2 minutes on the other side.
- Continue this process until all the batter is used, stacking the cooked crepes on a plate.

Fill and Roll the Crepes:
- Place a spoonful of the cheese filling on one half of each crepe.
- Fold the crepe over the filling, creating a half-moon shape, and then fold it again to form a triangle.

Serve:
- Arrange the filled and rolled crepes on a serving platter.
- Dust the crepes with powdered sugar.
- Optionally, serve with fruit preserves or syrup on the side.

Enjoy:
- Naleśniki z Serem are best enjoyed warm. Serve them for breakfast, dessert, or as a sweet snack.

These cheese-filled crepes are a delightful combination of thin pancakes and a sweet, creamy cheese filling. They're a beloved treat in Polish cuisine and are sure to be a hit at your table.

# Polish Main Courses:

**Ryba po Grecku (Fish Greek Style)**

Ingredients:

- 1 kg (2.2 lbs) white fish fillets (such as cod or haddock)
- 2 large onions, finely chopped
- 4-5 medium-sized carrots, grated
- 1 celery root, grated
- 1 cup tomato passata or crushed tomatoes
- 1/4 cup tomato paste
- 1/2 cup vegetable or fish broth
- 1/4 cup olive oil
- 2 bay leaves
- 1 teaspoon sugar
- 1 teaspoon sweet paprika
- Salt and pepper to taste
- Fresh parsley, chopped (for garnish)

Instructions:

Preheat your oven to 180°C (350°F).
In a large pan, sauté the chopped onions in olive oil until they become translucent.
Add grated carrots and celery root to the pan. Continue to cook for about 5-7 minutes until the vegetables soften.
Stir in the tomato passata, tomato paste, vegetable or fish broth, bay leaves, sugar, sweet paprika, salt, and pepper. Mix well and let it simmer for another 5-10 minutes.
Place the fish fillets in a baking dish and pour the vegetable and tomato mixture over them, making sure the fish is well coated.
Cover the baking dish with aluminum foil and bake in the preheated oven for about 30-40 minutes or until the fish is cooked through and flakes easily.
Once cooked, remove the bay leaves and garnish with chopped fresh parsley.
Serve the Fish Greek Style hot with your favorite side dishes, such as boiled potatoes or crusty bread.

This dish is known for its rich and savory flavors, and the combination of vegetables and spices adds a Greek-inspired twist to the preparation of fish. Enjoy your Ryba po Grecku!

**Kurczak Pieczony (Roast Chicken)**

Ingredients:

- 1 whole chicken (about 3-4 lbs)
- 2 tablespoons olive oil
- 2 teaspoons salt
- 1 teaspoon black pepper
- 1 teaspoon paprika
- 1 teaspoon dried thyme
- 1 teaspoon garlic powder
- 1 teaspoon onion powder
- 1 lemon, cut into halves
- Fresh herbs (such as rosemary or thyme), optional for stuffing
- Vegetables (carrots, potatoes, onions) for roasting, optional

Instructions:

Preheat your oven to 200°C (400°F).

Rinse the whole chicken inside and out under cold running water. Pat it dry with paper towels.

In a small bowl, mix together olive oil, salt, black pepper, paprika, dried thyme, garlic powder, and onion powder to create a seasoning rub.

Rub the seasoning mixture all over the chicken, ensuring it's evenly coated on all sides.

If desired, stuff the cavity of the chicken with lemon halves and fresh herbs for added flavor.

Optional: Place the seasoned chicken on a roasting pan and surround it with your choice of vegetables.

Roast the chicken in the preheated oven for about 1 to 1.5 hours or until the internal temperature reaches 75°C (165°F) and the skin is golden brown and crispy.

If the skin is browning too quickly, you can tent the chicken with aluminum foil to prevent it from burning.

Once cooked, remove the chicken from the oven and let it rest for 10-15 minutes before carving.

Carve the chicken into serving portions and serve it with your favorite side dishes.

This simple roast chicken recipe results in a flavorful and juicy dish, perfect for a family meal or a special occasion. Feel free to customize the seasonings or add your favorite herbs and spices to suit your taste. Enjoy your Kurczak Pieczony!

**Placek Ziemniaczany**

Ingredients:

- 4 large potatoes, peeled and grated
- 1 onion, grated
- 2 eggs
- 3 tablespoons all-purpose flour
- Salt and pepper to taste
- Oil for frying

Instructions:

Grate the peeled potatoes and onion. You can use a box grater or a food processor for this.

Place the grated potatoes and onion in a clean kitchen towel or cheesecloth and squeeze out as much liquid as possible.

In a bowl, combine the grated potatoes and onion with eggs, flour, salt, and pepper. Mix well to form a batter.

Heat oil in a frying pan over medium-high heat.

Spoon portions of the batter into the hot oil, spreading them into pancake shapes. Cook until golden brown on both sides, about 3-4 minutes per side.

Remove the pancakes from the pan and place them on a plate lined with paper towels to absorb any excess oil.

Repeat the process until all the batter is used.

Serve the Highlander Potato Pancakes hot with your favorite toppings. Traditional toppings include sour cream or applesauce.

These potato pancakes are a classic dish in Polish cuisine and are enjoyed in various regions, including the highlander areas. They are simple to make and have a delicious, comforting flavor. If you were looking for a different dish, please provide more details or a correct name, and I'd be happy to help!

**Jagnięcina Pieczona (Roast Lamb)**

Ingredients:

- 1 leg of lamb (about 4-5 pounds)
- 4 cloves of garlic, minced
- 2 tablespoons fresh rosemary, chopped
- 2 tablespoons fresh thyme, chopped
- 2 tablespoons olive oil
- 1 teaspoon salt
- 1/2 teaspoon black pepper
- 1 cup chicken or vegetable broth
- 1/2 cup dry white wine (optional)
- 2 tablespoons flour (for gravy, optional)

Instructions:

Preheat your oven to 180°C (350°F).

Make small incisions all over the leg of lamb with a sharp knife.

In a small bowl, mix together the minced garlic, chopped rosemary, chopped thyme, olive oil, salt, and black pepper to create a paste.

Rub the garlic and herb paste all over the leg of lamb, making sure to get it into the incisions.

Place the lamb on a roasting rack in a roasting pan, fat side up.

Pour the chicken or vegetable broth into the bottom of the roasting pan. You can also add white wine for extra flavor if you like.

Roast the lamb in the preheated oven for about 20 minutes per pound, or until the internal temperature reaches your desired doneness (medium-rare is about 57-60°C or 135-140°F, medium is around 63-68°C or 145-155°F).

Baste the lamb with the pan juices every 30 minutes to keep it moist.

Once cooked to your liking, remove the lamb from the oven and let it rest for about 15-20 minutes before carving.

Optional: To make gravy, transfer the pan juices to a saucepan. Whisk in flour until smooth, and cook over medium heat until thickened.

Carve the lamb into slices and serve it with the optional gravy and your favorite side dishes.

This roast lamb recipe results in a flavorful and tender dish that's perfect for special occasions or holiday meals. Enjoy your Jagnięcina Pieczona!

**Karp smażony (Fried Carp)**

Ingredients:

- 1 carp fish (cleaned and scaled), about 2-3 pounds
- 1 cup all-purpose flour
- Salt and pepper to taste
- 2 eggs, beaten
- Vegetable oil for frying
- Lemon wedges (for serving)
- Optional: Fresh dill for garnish

Instructions:

Rinse the carp thoroughly under cold running water and pat it dry with paper towels. Make sure the fish is clean and free of scales.

Cut the carp into serving-sized pieces. If you bought the fish whole, you can have it filleted or cut into steaks.

Season the carp pieces with salt and pepper.

Place the flour in a shallow dish. Dip each carp piece into the beaten eggs, ensuring it's fully coated, and then dredge it in the flour, shaking off any excess.

Heat vegetable oil in a frying pan over medium heat. You'll need enough oil to cover the bottom of the pan.

Fry the carp pieces in batches until they are golden brown on both sides. Cooking time will depend on the thickness of the fish pieces, but it's typically around 4-6 minutes per side.

Once fried, place the carp on a plate lined with paper towels to absorb any excess oil.

Serve the Fried Carp hot, garnished with lemon wedges and fresh dill if desired. Enjoy the dish with your favorite side dishes, such as boiled potatoes, sautéed vegetables, or a simple salad.

Fried Carp is a classic Polish dish, and it's often enjoyed as part of the Wigilia (Christmas Eve) meal. The crispy coating and tender fish make it a delightful treat.

**Kaczka Pieczona (Roast Duck)**

Ingredients:

- 1 whole duck (about 4-5 pounds)
- Salt and pepper to taste
- 1 teaspoon dried thyme
- 1 teaspoon dried rosemary
- 1 teaspoon paprika
- 1 onion, quartered
- 2-3 cloves of garlic, peeled and smashed
- 1 orange or apple, halved
- 2 cups chicken or vegetable broth
- 1/2 cup dry white wine (optional)

Instructions:

Preheat your oven to 180°C (350°F).
Rinse the duck inside and out under cold running water. Pat it dry with paper towels.
Season the duck generously with salt, pepper, dried thyme, dried rosemary, and paprika, rubbing the seasonings both inside and outside the duck.
Place the quartered onion, smashed garlic cloves, and halved orange or apple inside the cavity of the duck. This will help infuse flavor during roasting.
If using, pour the white wine into the bottom of the roasting pan. Add the chicken or vegetable broth.
Place the seasoned duck on a rack in a roasting pan, breast side up.
Roast the duck in the preheated oven for about 2 to 2.5 hours, or until the internal temperature reaches at least 74°C (165°F) in the thickest part of the thigh.
Baste the duck with pan juices every 30 minutes to ensure it stays moist and flavorful.
If the skin is getting too brown, you can cover it loosely with aluminum foil.
Once cooked, remove the duck from the oven and let it rest for about 15-20 minutes before carving.
Carve the duck into serving portions and serve it with the pan juices as a gravy.

Roast Duck is a flavorful and festive dish, often enjoyed during special occasions and holidays. It pairs well with a variety of side dishes, such as roasted vegetables, potatoes, or a simple salad. Enjoy your Kaczka Pieczona!

**Pieczeń Wieprzowa (Roast Pork)**

Ingredients:

- 1 pork roast (about 3-4 pounds)
- Salt and pepper to taste
- 2 teaspoons dried marjoram
- 2 teaspoons caraway seeds (optional)
- 3 cloves of garlic, minced
- 2 tablespoons olive oil
- 1 onion, sliced
- 1 cup chicken or vegetable broth
- 1/2 cup dry white wine (optional)

Instructions:

Preheat your oven to 180°C (350°F).
Rinse the pork roast under cold running water and pat it dry with paper towels.
Season the pork roast with salt, pepper, dried marjoram, and caraway seeds (if using), rubbing the seasonings evenly over the surface.
Make small incisions in the pork and insert minced garlic into these cuts.
In a large ovenproof pan or roasting pan, heat olive oil over medium-high heat.
Sear the pork roast on all sides until browned.
Remove the pork from the pan and set it aside. In the same pan, sauté the sliced onion until softened.
Place the seared pork back into the pan with the onions.
If using, pour the white wine over the pork, and then add the chicken or vegetable broth to the pan.
Transfer the pan to the preheated oven and roast the pork for about 1.5 to 2 hours, or until the internal temperature reaches at least 63°C (145°F).
Baste the pork with the pan juices every 30 minutes to keep it moist.
Once cooked, remove the pork from the oven and let it rest for about 15-20 minutes before carving.
Carve the pork roast into slices and serve it with the pan juices as a gravy.

Roast Pork is a classic and flavorful dish, and it pairs well with various side dishes such as mashed potatoes, roasted vegetables, or sauerkraut. Enjoy your Pieczeń Wieprzowa!

## Kurczak duszony w Piwie (Beer-Braised Chicken)

Ingredients:

- 1 whole chicken, cut into serving pieces
- Salt and pepper to taste
- 2 tablespoons vegetable oil
- 1 onion, chopped
- 2 carrots, sliced
- 2 cloves garlic, minced
- 2 bay leaves
- 1 teaspoon dried thyme
- 1 teaspoon paprika
- 1 bottle (12 oz) of your favorite beer (pale ale or lager works well)
- 1 cup chicken broth
- 2 tablespoons all-purpose flour (optional, for thickening)

Instructions:

Season the chicken pieces with salt and pepper.

In a large, oven-safe pot or Dutch oven, heat the vegetable oil over medium-high heat. Brown the chicken pieces on all sides. Work in batches if needed to avoid overcrowding the pot.

Remove the browned chicken from the pot and set it aside.

In the same pot, add chopped onion, sliced carrots, and minced garlic. Sauté until the vegetables are softened.

Return the browned chicken to the pot. Add bay leaves, dried thyme, and paprika.

Pour in the beer and chicken broth, ensuring the chicken is partially submerged. Bring the liquid to a simmer.

Preheat your oven to 180°C (350°F).

If you want a thicker sauce, mix 2 tablespoons of flour with a bit of water to make a smooth paste. Stir the paste into the pot to thicken the sauce.

Cover the pot with a lid or foil and transfer it to the preheated oven.

Braise the chicken in the oven for about 1.5 to 2 hours, or until the chicken is tender and cooked through.

Optional: If you want a crispier skin, you can uncover the pot for the last 15-20 minutes of cooking.

Remove the pot from the oven, discard the bay leaves, and adjust the seasoning if necessary.

Serve the Beer-Braised Chicken with the flavorful sauce over mashed potatoes, rice, or crusty bread.

This dish has a rich and flavorful sauce from the combination of beer, chicken broth, and aromatic herbs. Enjoy your Kurczak duszony w Piwie!

**Pieczony Indyk (Roast Turkey)**

Ingredients:

- 1 whole turkey (12-15 pounds), thawed if frozen
- Salt and pepper to taste
- 1 cup unsalted butter, melted
- 1 tablespoon dried thyme
- 1 tablespoon dried rosemary
- 1 tablespoon dried sage
- 1 tablespoon garlic powder
- 1 onion, quartered
- 1 lemon, halved
- 4-6 cups chicken or turkey broth
- Optional: Vegetables for roasting (carrots, celery, onions)

Instructions:

Preheat your oven to 180°C (350°F).
Remove the turkey from the refrigerator and allow it to come to room temperature for about 30-60 minutes.
Rinse the turkey inside and out under cold running water. Pat it dry with paper towels.
Season the inside of the turkey cavity with salt and pepper.
In a small bowl, mix together melted butter, dried thyme, dried rosemary, dried sage, and garlic powder.
Carefully loosen the skin over the turkey breast and rub half of the herb butter mixture under the skin. Rub the remaining mixture over the outside of the turkey.
Place the quartered onion and halved lemon inside the turkey cavity.
If desired, truss the turkey legs with kitchen twine.
Place the turkey on a rack in a roasting pan. If you like, surround the turkey with vegetables for added flavor.
Pour 2-3 cups of chicken or turkey broth into the bottom of the roasting pan.
Roast the turkey in the preheated oven, basting every 30 minutes with the pan juices and additional broth, until the internal temperature reaches 75°C (165°F). Cooking time will vary depending on the size of the turkey.
If the skin is browning too quickly, you can cover it loosely with aluminum foil.

Once the turkey is done, remove it from the oven and let it rest for at least 20-30 minutes before carving.
Carve the turkey into slices and serve it with your favorite sides.

Roast Turkey is often served with classic accompaniments like stuffing, cranberry sauce, and gravy. Enjoy your Pieczony Indyk!

**Cielecina duszona z Warzywami (Veal Stew)**

Ingredients:

- 1.5 pounds (about 700g) veal stew meat, cut into cubes
- 2 tablespoons vegetable oil
- 1 onion, finely chopped
- 2 carrots, peeled and sliced
- 2 celery stalks, sliced
- 2 cloves garlic, minced
- 2 tablespoons all-purpose flour
- 1 cup dry white wine
- 2 cups beef or vegetable broth
- 1 bay leaf
- 1 teaspoon dried thyme
- Salt and pepper to taste
- 1 cup green peas (fresh or frozen)
- Chopped fresh parsley for garnish

Instructions:

In a large pot or Dutch oven, heat the vegetable oil over medium-high heat. Add the veal cubes and brown them on all sides. Work in batches if needed to avoid overcrowding the pot. Remove the browned veal and set it aside.
In the same pot, add chopped onion, sliced carrots, sliced celery, and minced garlic. Sauté until the vegetables are softened.
Stir in the flour and cook for 1-2 minutes to eliminate the raw flour taste.
Pour in the dry white wine, scraping the bottom of the pot to deglaze and incorporate any flavorful bits.
Add the browned veal back to the pot.
Pour in the beef or vegetable broth, add the bay leaf, dried thyme, salt, and pepper. Bring the mixture to a simmer.
Reduce the heat to low, cover the pot, and let it simmer gently for about 1.5 to 2 hours or until the veal is tender.
About 30 minutes before the end of cooking, add the green peas.
Taste and adjust the seasoning if necessary.
Once the veal is tender and the flavors have melded, remove the bay leaf.
Serve the veal stew hot, garnished with chopped fresh parsley.

This Veal Stew with Vegetables is a hearty and comforting dish. You can enjoy it on its own or serve it with crusty bread, rice, or mashed potatoes. Bon appétit!

# Polish Side Dishes:

**Kasza Gryczana (Buckwheat Groats)**

Ingredients:

- 1 cup buckwheat groats
- 2 cups water or broth
- Salt to taste

Instructions:

Rinse the buckwheat groats under cold running water. This helps remove any excess starch and prevents the groats from becoming too sticky during cooking.
In a medium saucepan, combine the rinsed buckwheat groats and water or broth. Add a pinch of salt to taste.
Bring the mixture to a boil over high heat.
Once boiling, reduce the heat to low, cover the saucepan with a lid, and simmer for about 10-15 minutes or until the buckwheat is tender. You can check for doneness by tasting a few groats.
Once the buckwheat is cooked, remove the saucepan from the heat and let it sit, covered, for an additional 5 minutes. This allows the groats to absorb any remaining liquid and fluff up.
After the resting period, use a fork to fluff the buckwheat groats, separating any that may have stuck together during cooking.
Serve the cooked buckwheat groats as a side dish, in salads, or as a base for various savory or sweet dishes.

Buckwheat groats have a nutty flavor and a slightly chewy texture. They are gluten-free and rich in nutrients. You can customize the dish by adding herbs, spices, or sautéed vegetables to enhance the flavor. Buckwheat groats are a great alternative to rice or other grains, and they pair well with a variety of dishes. Enjoy your Kasza Gryczana!

**Placki Ziemniaczane z Gulaszem (Potato Pancakes with Goulash)**

Ingredients:

- 4 large potatoes, peeled and grated
- 1 onion, grated
- 2 eggs, beaten
- 3 tablespoons all-purpose flour
- Salt and pepper to taste
- Vegetable oil for frying

Instructions:

Place the grated potatoes in a clean kitchen towel and squeeze out as much liquid as possible.

In a bowl, combine the grated potatoes, grated onion, beaten eggs, flour, salt, and pepper. Mix well to form a batter.

Heat vegetable oil in a frying pan over medium heat.

Spoon portions of the batter into the hot oil, spreading them into pancake shapes. Cook until golden brown on both sides, about 3-4 minutes per side.

Place the cooked potato pancakes on a plate lined with paper towels to absorb any excess oil.

**Goulash (Gulasz):**

Ingredients:

- 1.5 pounds (about 700g) beef stew meat, cut into cubes
- 2 tablespoons vegetable oil
- 2 onions, chopped
- 2 cloves garlic, minced
- 2 tablespoons sweet paprika
- 1 teaspoon caraway seeds
- 1 bell pepper, diced
- 1 can (14 oz) diced tomatoes
- 2 cups beef broth
- Salt and pepper to taste

Instructions:

In a large pot or Dutch oven, heat vegetable oil over medium-high heat.
Add the beef cubes and brown them on all sides. Remove the browned beef and set it aside.
In the same pot, add chopped onions and sauté until softened.
Add minced garlic, sweet paprika, and caraway seeds. Cook for an additional 2 minutes.
Return the browned beef to the pot. Add diced bell pepper, diced tomatoes, and beef broth. Season with salt and pepper to taste.
Bring the mixture to a simmer, then reduce the heat to low. Cover the pot and let it simmer for about 1.5 to 2 hours or until the beef is tender.
Adjust the seasoning if necessary before serving.

Serve the Goulash over the Potato Pancakes, and you have a comforting and flavorful Polish meal. You can also garnish with fresh herbs like parsley if desired. Enjoy your Placki Ziemniaczane z Gulaszem!

**Kopytka (Potato Dumplings)**

Ingredients:

- 4 large potatoes, peeled and boiled until tender
- 2 cups all-purpose flour
- 1 egg
- Salt to taste

Instructions:

Mash the boiled potatoes while they are still warm. You can use a potato masher or pass them through a potato ricer for a smoother texture.

In a large mixing bowl, combine the mashed potatoes with the flour, egg, and a pinch of salt. Mix well until a dough forms.

Knead the dough on a floured surface for a few minutes until it becomes smooth.

Divide the dough into smaller portions. Roll each portion into a long rope, about 1/2 inch in diameter.

Cut the ropes into small pieces, each about the size of a thumbprint.

Optional: Create a slight indentation in the middle of each dumpling with your thumb or the back of a fork. This step gives them their characteristic shape.

Bring a large pot of salted water to a boil.

Drop the dumplings into the boiling water and cook until they float to the surface. This usually takes 3-5 minutes.

Using a slotted spoon, remove the dumplings from the water and place them on a plate.

Serve the Kopytka hot with your favorite sauce or topping. They go well with melted butter, sautéed onions, or a simple tomato sauce. Enjoy your homemade Kopytka!

**Ziemniaki Puree (Mashed Potatoes)**

Ingredients:

- 4 large potatoes, peeled and cut into chunks
- 1/2 cup (1 stick) unsalted butter
- 1/2 to 1 cup milk (adjust to desired consistency)
- Salt and pepper to taste
- Optional: Chopped fresh parsley for garnish

Instructions:

Place the potato chunks in a large pot and cover them with cold water. Add a pinch of salt to the water.
Bring the water to a boil over high heat, then reduce the heat to medium and simmer until the potatoes are fork-tender. This usually takes about 15-20 minutes.
Drain the potatoes thoroughly.
In a separate small saucepan, melt the butter over low heat. Add the milk to the melted butter and warm it but avoid boiling.
Using a potato masher or a ricer, mash the cooked potatoes in a large bowl. Gradually add the warm butter and milk mixture to the mashed potatoes, blending continuously until you achieve the desired creamy consistency. Adjust the amount of milk based on your preference for creaminess.
Season the mashed potatoes with salt and pepper to taste. Mix well.
Optional: Garnish with chopped fresh parsley for added flavor and a pop of color.

Serve the Ziemniaki Puree hot alongside your favorite main dishes. Mashed potatoes are versatile and can complement anything from roasted meats to vegetarian dishes.

Enjoy your creamy and delicious mashed potatoes!

**Kluski Śląskie (Silesian Dumplings)**

Ingredients:

- 4 large starchy potatoes (such as Russet potatoes)
- 1 cup potato starch
- 1 cup all-purpose flour
- 1 teaspoon salt
- Optional: 1 egg (for added richness)

Instructions:

Peel and boil the potatoes until they are fully cooked. You can check their doneness by inserting a fork; they should be soft.

Mash the boiled potatoes while they are still warm. You can use a potato masher or pass them through a potato ricer for a smoother texture.

Let the mashed potatoes cool to room temperature.

In a large mixing bowl, combine the mashed potatoes with potato starch, all-purpose flour, and salt. If you choose to use an egg, add it to the mixture.

Knead the dough until it is smooth. The dough should be soft and pliable but not sticky. If it's too sticky, you can add a bit more potato starch.

Divide the dough into smaller portions.

Roll each portion into a rope on a floured surface, then cut the rope into smaller pieces, forming individual dumplings. You can also shape them into small, flat discs.

Bring a large pot of salted water to a gentle boil.

Drop the dumplings into the boiling water, and cook until they float to the surface. This usually takes 5-7 minutes.

Using a slotted spoon, remove the dumplings from the water and place them on a plate.

Serve the Kluski Śląskie hot with your favorite sauce or topping. They pair well with various meats, stews, or sauces. Enjoy your homemade Silesian Dumplings!

**Kiszona Kapusta (Pickled Cabbage)**

Ingredients:

- 1 medium-sized head of cabbage (green or white)
- 2-3 carrots, peeled and grated (optional)
- 2 tablespoons coarse salt (pickling salt or sea salt)
- 1-2 teaspoons caraway seeds (optional)
- Water

Instructions:

Prepare the Cabbage:
- Remove the outer leaves of the cabbage and save them for later.
- Cut the cabbage into quarters and remove the core.
- Thinly slice the cabbage into shreds using a sharp knife or a mandoline.

Combine with Salt:
- Place the shredded cabbage in a large mixing bowl.
- Sprinkle the salt over the cabbage and start massaging and squeezing it with your hands. This helps release the cabbage juices and begins the fermentation process.
- If using, add grated carrots and caraway seeds to the cabbage.

Pack into a Jar:
- Take handfuls of the salted and massaged cabbage and pack them tightly into a clean, sterilized glass jar. Press down as you go to remove air pockets.
- Pour any released cabbage juice into the jar.

Use Outer Cabbage Leaves:
- Take the saved outer cabbage leaves and place them over the shredded cabbage in the jar. These leaves will act as a barrier to keep the shredded cabbage submerged in its own juices.

Weigh Down:
- Place a weight on top of the cabbage to ensure it stays submerged. You can use a clean, sanitized rock, a smaller jar filled with water, or any other food-safe weight.

Cover and Ferment:
- Cover the jar with a clean cloth or muslin and secure it with a rubber band or string. This allows air to circulate while keeping out dust and debris.
- Place the jar in a cool, dark place to ferment. Check it daily to ensure the cabbage remains submerged.

Taste and Store:
- Taste the pickled cabbage after a few days to check its flavor. Once it reaches your desired level of fermentation, remove the outer leaves and store the jar in the refrigerator.

Your homemade Kiszona Kapusta is ready to be enjoyed as a tangy and crunchy side dish or as an ingredient in various recipes like Bigos (Hunter's Stew) or Kapuśniak (Cabbage Soup).

## Kasza Manna (Semolina Porridge)

Ingredients:

- 1 cup semolina
- 3 cups milk
- 2 tablespoons sugar (adjust to taste)
- A pinch of salt
- Butter or your choice of toppings (honey, fruit, nuts) for serving

Instructions:

Heat the Milk:
- In a saucepan, heat the milk over medium heat until it comes to a gentle simmer. Be careful not to boil the milk.

Add Semolina:
- Gradually sprinkle the semolina into the simmering milk, stirring constantly to avoid lumps.

Cooking:
- Continue to cook the mixture over low to medium heat, stirring continuously. This helps the semolina absorb the milk and prevents clumps from forming.

Sweeten and Season:
- Add sugar and a pinch of salt to the porridge. Adjust the sweetness according to your preference.

Continue Cooking:
- Keep stirring and cooking the porridge until it thickens to your desired consistency. This usually takes about 5-7 minutes.

Serve:
- Once the semolina is fully cooked and the porridge has thickened, remove it from the heat.

Optional: Add Butter or Toppings:
- Stir in a knob of butter for added richness or customize your porridge with toppings like honey, maple syrup, fresh fruit, or nuts.

Serve Warm:
- Serve the Kasza Manna warm in bowls. It can be enjoyed for breakfast, as a dessert, or a comforting snack.

Semolina porridge is versatile, and you can experiment with different flavors and textures by adding your favorite ingredients. Adjust the sugar and toppings to suit your taste preferences, and enjoy this cozy and nourishing dish!

## Kopytka (Potato Dumplings)

Ingredients:

- 4 large potatoes, peeled and boiled until tender
- 2 cups all-purpose flour
- 1 egg
- Salt to taste
- Butter or oil for frying

Instructions:

> Prepare Potatoes:
> - Peel and boil the potatoes until they are tender. Drain them and let them cool for a bit.
>
> Mash Potatoes:
> - Mash the boiled potatoes while they are still warm. You can use a potato masher or pass them through a potato ricer for a smoother texture.
>
> Combine Ingredients:
> - In a large mixing bowl, combine the mashed potatoes with flour, egg, and a pinch of salt. Mix well until a dough forms.
>
> Knead the Dough:
> - Knead the dough on a floured surface for a few minutes until it becomes smooth. If the dough is too sticky, add a bit more flour.
>
> Form Dumplings:
> - Divide the dough into smaller portions. Roll each portion into a rope, about 1/2 inch in diameter.
>
> Cut into Pieces:
> - Cut the ropes into small pieces, forming individual dumplings. You can shape them into small, flat discs or oval shapes resembling hooves ("kopytka" translates to hooves in English).
>
> Boil Dumplings:
> - Bring a large pot of salted water to a boil.
> - Drop the dumplings into the boiling water and cook until they float to the surface. This usually takes 3-5 minutes.
>
> Fry Dumplings (Optional):
> - After boiling, you can fry the dumplings in a pan with butter or oil until they get a golden brown crust on the outside. This step is optional but adds a delicious flavor.
>
> Serve:

- Serve the Kopytka hot as a side dish. They pair well with various sauces, sautéed onions, or simply butter.

Enjoy your homemade Kopytka! They are a delightful and comforting addition to any meal.

## Kiszony Ogórek (Pickles)

Ingredients:

- 2-3 pounds small pickling cucumbers
- 4 cups water
- 1/2 cup salt
- 1-2 heads of fresh dill
- 4-6 cloves of garlic, peeled
- 1 tablespoon mustard seeds (optional)
- 1 teaspoon whole black peppercorns (optional)
- 1-2 dried red chili peppers (optional)
- Cherry leaves or grape leaves (optional, for crispiness)
- Additional herbs and spices to taste (coriander, bay leaves, etc.)

Instructions:

Prepare Cucumbers:
- Wash the cucumbers thoroughly. Trim the ends and, if desired, slice them into halves or spears.

Create Brine:
- In a large bowl, dissolve salt in water to create a brine.

Soak Cucumbers:
- Place the cucumbers in the brine. Use a plate or other weight to keep them submerged. Let them soak for 12-24 hours.

Rinse Cucumbers:
- After soaking, rinse the cucumbers under cold water to remove excess salt.

Prepare Jars:
- Sterilize your jars by boiling them in water or running them through a dishwasher.

Layer Ingredients:
- In each sterilized jar, layer fresh dill, peeled garlic cloves, mustard seeds, black peppercorns, chili peppers, and any additional herbs and spices you like.

Pack Jars:
- Pack the jars tightly with the rinsed cucumbers.

Add Grape or Cherry Leaves (Optional):

- If you have access to them, add grape leaves or cherry leaves to the jars. These leaves contain tannins, which help maintain the crispiness of the pickles.

Boil Brine:
- In a saucepan, bring water to a boil. Allow it to cool slightly before pouring it into the jars.

Fill Jars:
- Fill the jars with the hot brine, covering the cucumbers completely.

Seal Jars:
- Seal the jars tightly. Let them cool to room temperature.

Ferment:
- Place the sealed jars in a cool, dark place and allow them to ferment for about 1-2 weeks. Check the pickles regularly and taste them until they reach the desired level of sourness.

Store:
- Once fermented, store the pickles in the refrigerator to slow down the fermentation process.

Enjoy your homemade Kiszony Ogórek! These pickles make a tasty and traditional addition to sandwiches, salads, or as a flavorful snack.

## Marchewka z Groszkiem (Carrots with Peas)

Ingredients:

- 4 large carrots, peeled and sliced into thin rounds
- 1 cup frozen peas
- 1 small onion, finely chopped
- 2 tablespoons butter or vegetable oil
- Salt and pepper to taste
- Fresh dill for garnish (optional)

Instructions:

Prepare Carrots:
- Peel the carrots and slice them into thin rounds.

Cook Carrots:
- In a saucepan, bring water to a boil. Add a pinch of salt and cook the carrot slices until they are tender but still have a slight crunch. This usually takes about 5-7 minutes.

Cook Peas:
- In the last 2 minutes of cooking the carrots, add the frozen peas to the boiling water. Cook until the peas are heated through.

Drain Vegetables:
- Drain the carrots and peas in a colander and set them aside.

Sauté Onion:
- In a separate pan, heat butter or vegetable oil over medium heat. Add finely chopped onion and sauté until it becomes translucent.

Combine and Season:
- Add the drained carrots and peas to the sautéed onions. Mix well to combine. Season with salt and pepper to taste.

Garnish:
- If desired, garnish the dish with fresh dill for added flavor and a pop of color.

Serve:
- Serve Marchewka z Groszkiem hot as a delightful and colorful side dish.

This dish is a staple in Polish cuisine and is often served alongside meat dishes or as part of a vegetarian meal. The combination of sweet carrots and vibrant green peas makes it visually appealing, and the flavors are enhanced by the sautéed onions and butter. Enjoy your Carrots with Peas!

# Polish Desserts:

**Sernik (Cheesecake)**

Ingredients:

For the Crust:

- 2 cups graham cracker crumbs
- 1/2 cup unsalted butter, melted
- 2 tablespoons sugar

For the Filling:

- 4 cups farmer's cheese or dry-curd cottage cheese (pressed to remove excess moisture)
- 1 cup sugar
- 4 large eggs
- 1/2 cup sour cream
- 1/4 cup all-purpose flour
- 1 teaspoon vanilla extract
- Zest of 1 lemon
- Pinch of salt

For the Topping (optional):

- Fruit preserves or fresh fruit for topping (cherry or raspberry preserves are common)

Instructions:

    Preheat the Oven:
- Preheat your oven to 325°F (160°C).

    Prepare the Crust:
- In a bowl, combine the graham cracker crumbs, melted butter, and sugar. Mix until the crumbs are evenly coated.
- Press the mixture into the bottom of a greased 9-inch (23 cm) springform pan, creating an even crust. You can use the back of a spoon to press it down firmly.
- Place the pan in the refrigerator to chill while you prepare the filling.

    Prepare the Filling:

- In a large mixing bowl, blend the farmer's cheese (or dry-curd cottage cheese) until smooth. You can use a food processor or an electric mixer for this.
- Add sugar, eggs, sour cream, flour, vanilla extract, lemon zest, and a pinch of salt. Mix until well combined and smooth.

Pour into the Crust:
- Take the chilled crust from the refrigerator and pour the cheesecake filling over it.

Bake:
- Bake in the preheated oven for about 1 hour or until the center is set and the top is lightly golden.

Cool and Refrigerate:
- Allow the cheesecake to cool in the pan on a wire rack. Once it reaches room temperature, refrigerate it for several hours or preferably overnight to allow it to set completely.

Add Topping (Optional):
- If desired, spread a layer of fruit preserves or fresh fruit on top of the chilled cheesecake before serving.

Serve:
- Release the sides of the springform pan and transfer the cheesecake to a serving plate. Slice and serve.

Enjoy your homemade Sernik! Polish cheesecake is rich and creamy, and its flavor develops even more as it chills in the refrigerator.

**Makowiec (Poppy Seed Roll)**

Ingredients:

For the Dough:

- 4 cups all-purpose flour
- 1/2 cup unsalted butter, softened
- 1/2 cup granulated sugar
- 2 large eggs
- 1 cup milk, lukewarm
- 1 tablespoon active dry yeast
- 1/4 teaspoon salt

For the Filling:

- 1 1/2 cups ground poppy seeds
- 1 cup milk
- 1/2 cup granulated sugar
- 1/4 cup honey
- 1/4 cup unsalted butter
- Zest of 1 lemon
- 1/2 cup raisins (optional)
- 1/2 cup chopped nuts (walnuts or almonds), toasted

Additional:

- 1 egg, beaten (for egg wash)
- Powdered sugar (for dusting)

Instructions:

Prepare the Dough:

> In a small bowl, combine lukewarm milk with sugar and yeast. Let it sit for about 10 minutes until frothy.
> In a large mixing bowl, cream together softened butter, sugar, and eggs.
> Add the yeast mixture to the creamed mixture and mix well.
> Gradually add flour and salt to form a soft dough. Knead the dough on a floured surface until smooth.

Place the dough in a greased bowl, cover it with a kitchen towel, and let it rise in a warm place for about 1-2 hours or until doubled in size.

Prepare the Filling:

In a saucepan, combine ground poppy seeds, milk, sugar, honey, butter, and lemon zest.
Cook the mixture over medium heat, stirring constantly, until it thickens. This usually takes about 10-15 minutes.
Remove the filling from heat and let it cool. Stir in raisins and chopped nuts.

Assemble the Makowiec:

Preheat your oven to 350°F (180°C).
Punch down the risen dough and roll it out on a floured surface into a large rectangle.
Spread the poppy seed filling evenly over the rolled-out dough.
Roll the dough tightly from the longer side, creating a log shape.
Place the rolled dough on a parchment-lined baking sheet, seam side down.
Brush the top of the roll with beaten egg for a shiny finish.
Bake in the preheated oven for about 30-40 minutes or until golden brown.
Allow the Makowiec to cool completely before slicing.
Dust the top with powdered sugar before serving.

Enjoy your homemade Makowiec, a delightful Polish poppy seed roll that's perfect for festive occasions!

**Kremówka Papieska (Papal Cream Cake)**

Ingredients:

For the Puff Pastry Layers:

- 2 sheets of puff pastry (store-bought or homemade)
- Powdered sugar for dusting

For the Cream Filling:

- 2 cups whole milk
- 1 cup heavy cream
- 1 cup granulated sugar
- 1/2 cup cornstarch
- 6 large egg yolks
- 1 teaspoon vanilla extract
- 1/4 cup unsalted butter, softened

Instructions:

Prepare the Puff Pastry Layers:

> Preheat your oven according to the instructions on the puff pastry package or to around 375°F (190°C).
> Roll out the puff pastry sheets on a floured surface, if needed, to fit a baking sheet.
> Place the rolled-out puff pastry sheets on a parchment-lined baking sheet.
> Prick the surface of the puff pastry with a fork to prevent excessive rising.
> Bake in the preheated oven until golden brown and puffed. Follow the baking time indicated on the puff pastry package or until the pastry is fully cooked.
> Once baked, allow the puff pastry layers to cool completely.

Prepare the Cream Filling:

> In a saucepan, combine milk, heavy cream, and sugar. Heat the mixture over medium heat until it just starts to simmer.
> In a separate bowl, whisk together egg yolks and cornstarch until well combined.
> Slowly pour the hot milk mixture into the egg yolk mixture, whisking constantly to avoid curdling.

Return the combined mixture to the saucepan and continue to cook over medium heat, stirring constantly, until the custard thickens.

Remove the custard from heat and stir in vanilla extract and softened butter. Mix until smooth.

Let the custard cool to room temperature, covering it with plastic wrap directly on the surface to prevent a skin from forming.

Assemble the Kremówka Papieska:

Once the puff pastry layers and custard are both cooled, place one puff pastry layer on a serving plate.

Spread a generous layer of the custard over the first puff pastry layer.

Place the second puff pastry layer on top.

Dust the top with powdered sugar.

Optionally, use a sharp knife to score the top layer into serving portions.

Refrigerate the Kremówka Papieska for a few hours or overnight to allow the flavors to meld and the dessert to set.

Slice and serve chilled.

Enjoy your Kremówka Papieska, a delightful and iconic Polish dessert!

## Pączki (Polish Doughnuts)

Ingredients:

For the Dough:

- 4 cups all-purpose flour
- 1 cup whole milk, lukewarm
- 1/2 cup unsalted butter, softened
- 1/4 cup granulated sugar
- 1 packet (2 1/4 teaspoons) active dry yeast
- 4 large egg yolks
- 1 teaspoon vanilla extract
- Zest of 1 lemon or orange (optional)
- Pinch of salt

For Frying:

- Vegetable oil for frying

For Filling and Topping (Optional):

- Fruit jam or preserves (plum, raspberry, rose hip, or your favorite flavor)
- Powdered sugar for dusting

Instructions:

Activate Yeast:
- In a small bowl, combine lukewarm milk, a pinch of sugar, and the active dry yeast. Let it sit for about 5-10 minutes until it becomes frothy.

Prepare Dough:
- In a large mixing bowl, combine the activated yeast mixture, flour, softened butter, sugar, egg yolks, vanilla extract, zest (if using), and a pinch of salt.
- Mix the ingredients until a soft dough forms.

Knead and Rise:
- Turn the dough out onto a floured surface and knead for about 5-7 minutes until it becomes smooth.
- Place the dough in a greased bowl, cover it with a kitchen towel, and let it rise in a warm place until doubled in size. This usually takes about 1-2 hours.

Roll and Cut:

- Roll out the risen dough on a floured surface to a thickness of about 1/2 inch.
- Use a round cutter to cut out doughnut shapes. Alternatively, you can use a glass for a round shape and a smaller cutter for the center hole.

Second Rise:
- Place the cut doughnuts on a floured surface or parchment paper, cover them with a kitchen towel, and let them rise for another 30-45 minutes.

Heat Oil:
- Heat vegetable oil in a deep fryer or a large, deep pan to 350-375°F (175-190°C).

Fry:
- Carefully place the risen doughnuts into the hot oil, a few at a time. Fry until golden brown on both sides, turning them halfway through. This usually takes about 2-3 minutes per side.

Drain and Cool:
- Use a slotted spoon to remove the fried doughnuts and place them on a paper towel-lined plate to absorb excess oil.
- Allow the doughnuts to cool completely.

Fill and Dust (Optional):
- Once cooled, you can fill the doughnuts with your favorite fruit jam or preserves using a pastry bag and a filling tip.
- Optionally, dust the filled or unfilled doughnuts with powdered sugar.

Enjoy your homemade Pączki! These Polish doughnuts are a delightful treat, especially when freshly fried and filled with your favorite jam.

**Babka (Easter Cake)**

Ingredients:

For the Dough:

- 4 cups all-purpose flour
- 1 cup unsalted butter, softened
- 1/2 cup granulated sugar
- 4 large eggs
- 1 cup whole milk, lukewarm
- 1 packet (2 1/4 teaspoons) active dry yeast
- Zest of 1 lemon or orange
- 1/2 teaspoon salt

For the Filling:

- 1 cup raisins (soaked in warm water or rum)
- 1/2 cup granulated sugar
- 2 teaspoons ground cinnamon
- 1 cup finely chopped nuts (walnuts or pecans)

For the Glaze (Optional):

- 1/2 cup powdered sugar
- 1-2 tablespoons milk
- 1/2 teaspoon vanilla extract

Instructions:

Activate Yeast:
- In a small bowl, combine lukewarm milk, a pinch of sugar, and the active dry yeast. Let it sit for about 5-10 minutes until it becomes frothy.

Prepare Dough:
- In a large mixing bowl, cream together softened butter and sugar until light and fluffy. Add eggs one at a time, beating well after each addition.
- Stir in the activated yeast mixture, zest, and salt.
- Gradually add the flour, mixing until a soft dough forms.

Knead and Rise:
- Turn the dough out onto a floured surface and knead for about 8-10 minutes until it becomes smooth and elastic.

- Place the dough in a greased bowl, cover it with a kitchen towel, and let it rise in a warm place until doubled in size. This usually takes about 1-2 hours.

Prepare Filling:
- In a bowl, mix together soaked and drained raisins, sugar, ground cinnamon, and chopped nuts.

Roll and Fill:
- Roll out the risen dough on a floured surface into a rectangle.
- Spread the filling evenly over the dough, leaving a small border around the edges.
- Roll the dough tightly from the longer side to form a log.

Shape the Babka:
- Place the rolled dough in a greased and floured bundt pan or a babka pan.
- Cover it with a kitchen towel and let it rise for an additional 30-45 minutes.

Bake:
- Preheat your oven to 350°F (180°C).
- Bake the babka in the preheated oven for about 30-40 minutes or until it's golden brown and sounds hollow when tapped.

Cool:
- Allow the babka to cool in the pan for about 15 minutes before transferring it to a wire rack to cool completely.

Prepare Glaze (Optional):
- If desired, mix powdered sugar, milk, and vanilla extract to make a glaze. Drizzle it over the cooled babka.

Slice and enjoy your homemade Babka! This sweet Easter cake is a wonderful addition to your holiday celebrations.

**Placuszki z Jabłkami (Apple Pancakes)**

Ingredients:

- 2 large apples, peeled, cored, and grated
- 1 cup all-purpose flour
- 1 teaspoon baking powder
- 2 tablespoons sugar
- 1/2 teaspoon cinnamon
- 1/2 cup milk
- 2 large eggs
- 1 teaspoon vanilla extract
- Pinch of salt
- Butter or oil for frying
- Powdered sugar for dusting (optional)
- Maple syrup or honey for serving (optional)

Instructions:

Prepare Apples:
- Peel, core, and grate the apples. Squeeze out excess moisture from the grated apples using a clean kitchen towel.

Prepare Batter:
- In a large bowl, whisk together flour, baking powder, sugar, cinnamon, and a pinch of salt.

Add Wet Ingredients:
- In a separate bowl, whisk together milk, eggs, and vanilla extract.

Combine Wet and Dry Ingredients:
- Pour the wet ingredients into the dry ingredients and mix until just combined. Do not overmix; a few lumps are okay.

Add Grated Apples:
- Gently fold the grated apples into the batter until evenly distributed.

Heat Pan:
- Heat a non-stick skillet or griddle over medium heat. Add a small amount of butter or oil to coat the surface.

Cook Pancakes:
- Drop spoonfuls of batter onto the hot skillet, spreading them slightly with the back of the spoon. Cook until bubbles form on the surface, then flip and cook the other side until golden brown.

Repeat:

- Repeat the process until all the batter is used. Add more butter or oil to the pan as needed.

Serve:
- Serve the apple pancakes warm. You can dust them with powdered sugar and drizzle with maple syrup or honey if desired.

Enjoy your Placuszki z Jabłkami! These apple pancakes are a delicious way to incorporate the natural sweetness of apples into a classic pancake recipe.

**Ciasto Drożdżowe z Owocami (Yeast Cake with Fruit)**

Ingredients:

For the Dough:

- 4 cups all-purpose flour
- 1/2 cup granulated sugar
- 1 packet (2 1/4 teaspoons) active dry yeast
- 1 cup warm milk
- 1/2 cup unsalted butter, melted
- 2 large eggs
- 1 teaspoon vanilla extract
- A pinch of salt

For the Fruit Topping:

- 2-3 cups of your favorite fruits (berries, sliced peaches, plums, apples, etc.)
- 1/4 cup granulated sugar
- 1 teaspoon ground cinnamon (optional)

Instructions:

Prepare the Dough:

> In a small bowl, combine warm milk, a pinch of sugar, and active dry yeast. Let it sit for about 5-10 minutes until it becomes frothy.
> In a large mixing bowl, whisk together flour, sugar, and salt.
> Make a well in the center of the flour mixture. Pour in the activated yeast mixture, melted butter, eggs, and vanilla extract.
> Mix the ingredients until a soft dough forms.
> Knead the dough on a floured surface for about 5-8 minutes until it becomes smooth and elastic.
> Place the dough in a greased bowl, cover it with a kitchen towel, and let it rise in a warm place until doubled in size. This usually takes about 1-2 hours.

Prepare the Fruit Topping:

> Wash and prepare your chosen fruits. If using apples or other fruits that may oxidize, you can toss them in a bit of lemon juice to prevent browning.
> In a bowl, gently toss the fruits with sugar. Add ground cinnamon if desired.

Assemble and Bake:

- Preheat your oven to 350°F (180°C).
- Punch down the risen dough and roll it out on a floured surface to fit a greased baking pan.
- Transfer the rolled-out dough to the baking pan.
- Arrange the prepared fruits over the dough, spreading them evenly.
- Bake in the preheated oven for about 25-30 minutes or until the crust is golden brown and the fruits are tender.
- Allow the yeast cake to cool in the pan before slicing.
- Optionally, dust with powdered sugar before serving.

Enjoy your homemade Ciasto Drożdżowe z Owocami! This yeast cake with fruit is a delightful combination of soft, sweet dough and the freshness of seasonal fruits.

**Kompot z Suszu (Dried Fruit Compote)**

Ingredients:

- 1 cup dried mixed fruits (such as apples, pears, plums, apricots, and raisins)
- 1/2 cup sugar (adjust to taste)
- 8-10 cups water
- 1 cinnamon stick (optional)
- 3-4 whole cloves (optional)
- Lemon or orange zest (optional)

Instructions:

Prepare Dried Fruits:
- Rinse the dried fruits under cold water to remove any dust or debris.

Soak the Dried Fruits:
- Place the dried fruits in a large bowl and cover them with water. Let them soak for at least 4 hours or overnight. This helps soften the fruits and enhances their flavor.

Cook Dried Fruits:
- In a large pot, combine the soaked dried fruits along with the soaking water.

Add Sugar and Spices:
- Add sugar to the pot. Adjust the amount based on your sweetness preference.
- If desired, add a cinnamon stick, whole cloves, and lemon or orange zest for additional flavor.

Bring to a Boil:
- Bring the mixture to a boil over medium-high heat, stirring occasionally.

Simmer:
- Once it reaches a boil, reduce the heat to low and let the compote simmer for about 30-45 minutes. This allows the flavors to meld, and the dried fruits to absorb the sweetness.

Taste and Adjust:
- Taste the compote and adjust the sweetness if needed by adding more sugar.

Cool:
- Allow the compote to cool to room temperature.

Strain (Optional):

- If you prefer a clear liquid, you can strain the compote to remove the fruit pieces. Otherwise, leave the fruits in for added texture.

Chill:
- Refrigerate the compote until it's well chilled.

Serve:
- Serve the Kompot z Suszu in glasses over ice, and enjoy it as a refreshing beverage.

Dried Fruit Compote is a versatile drink that can be served cold, making it a perfect choice for hot days, or warm during the colder seasons. It's a delicious way to enjoy the natural sweetness of dried fruits.

**Chałka (Sweet Bread)**

Ingredients:

For the Dough:

- 4 to 4 1/2 cups all-purpose flour
- 1/2 cup sugar
- 1 packet (2 1/4 teaspoons) active dry yeast
- 1 cup warm milk (about 110°F or 43°C)
- 1/2 cup unsalted butter, melted
- 3 large eggs
- 1 teaspoon vanilla extract
- 1/2 teaspoon salt

For the Egg Wash:

- 1 egg, beaten
- 1 tablespoon water

Optional Toppings:

- Sesame seeds or poppy seeds

Instructions:

Prepare the Dough:

In a small bowl, combine warm milk, a pinch of sugar, and active dry yeast. Let it sit for about 5-10 minutes until it becomes frothy.
In a large mixing bowl, combine 4 cups of flour, sugar, and salt.
Make a well in the center of the flour mixture. Pour in the activated yeast mixture, melted butter, eggs, and vanilla extract.
Mix the ingredients until a soft dough forms.
Knead the dough on a floured surface for about 8-10 minutes until it becomes smooth and elastic. If the dough is too sticky, add additional flour as needed.
Place the dough in a greased bowl, cover it with a kitchen towel, and let it rise in a warm place until doubled in size. This usually takes about 1-2 hours.

Shape and Bake:

Preheat your oven to 350°F (180°C). Line a baking sheet with parchment paper.

Punch down the risen dough and turn it out onto a floured surface.
Divide the dough into three equal parts. Roll each part into a long rope.
Braid the three ropes together, pinching the ends to seal.
Place the braided dough on the prepared baking sheet.
In a small bowl, whisk together the beaten egg and water to create an egg wash.
Brush the egg wash over the top of the braided dough.
Optionally, sprinkle sesame seeds or poppy seeds over the egg wash.
Bake in the preheated oven for about 25-30 minutes or until the bread is golden brown and sounds hollow when tapped.
Allow the Chałka to cool on a wire rack before slicing.

Enjoy your homemade Chałka! This sweet braided bread is a beautiful and delicious addition to festive meals and celebrations.

# Ciasto Kruche z Owocami (Shortcrust Pastry with Fruit)

Ingredients:

For the Shortcrust Pastry:

- 2 cups all-purpose flour
- 1/2 cup granulated sugar
- 1 cup unsalted butter, cold and cut into small cubes
- 1 large egg
- 1 teaspoon vanilla extract

For the Fruit Topping:

- 2-3 cups of your favorite fresh fruits (berries, sliced peaches, plums, apples, etc.)
- 1/4 cup apricot jam or fruit preserves for glazing

Instructions:

Prepare the Shortcrust Pastry:

In a food processor, combine flour and sugar.
Add the cold, cubed butter to the flour mixture. Pulse until the mixture resembles coarse crumbs.
In a small bowl, whisk together the egg and vanilla extract.
While pulsing the food processor, gradually add the egg mixture until the dough comes together. Be careful not to overmix.
Turn the dough out onto a floured surface and gently knead it into a ball. Flatten the ball into a disk, wrap it in plastic wrap, and refrigerate for at least 30 minutes.

Preheat your oven to 375°F (190°C).

Roll out the chilled dough on a floured surface to fit a tart or pie pan.
Carefully transfer the rolled-out dough to the pan, pressing it into the bottom and up the sides.

Prepare the Fruit Topping:

Arrange the fresh fruits over the prepared shortcrust pastry.
In a small saucepan, heat the apricot jam or fruit preserves over low heat until it becomes liquid.
Brush the melted jam over the arranged fruits for a shiny glaze.

Bake:

- Bake the tart in the preheated oven for about 25-30 minutes or until the crust is golden brown and the fruits are tender.
- Allow the tart to cool before serving.
- Optionally, you can dust the cooled tart with powdered sugar before serving.

Enjoy your Ciasto Kruche z Owocami! This shortcrust pastry with fruit is a delightful combination of buttery crust and the freshness of seasonal fruits.

# Polish Breads:

**Chleb Wiejski (Country Bread)**

Ingredients:

For the Starter (Poolish):

- 1 cup all-purpose flour
- 1/2 cup warm water
- 1/4 teaspoon active dry yeast

For the Dough:

- All of the starter (poolish) from the previous step
- 2 1/2 cups bread flour
- 1 cup whole wheat flour
- 1 1/2 teaspoons salt
- 1 cup warm water
- 1/4 teaspoon active dry yeast

Instructions:

Prepare the Starter (Poolish):

> In a bowl, combine 1 cup of all-purpose flour, 1/2 cup of warm water, and 1/4 teaspoon of active dry yeast.
> Mix until well combined. Cover the bowl with plastic wrap and let it sit at room temperature for at least 8 hours or overnight. This is your poolish starter.

Make the Dough:

> In a large mixing bowl, combine the poolish starter, 2 1/2 cups of bread flour, 1 cup of whole wheat flour, and 1 1/2 teaspoons of salt.
> In a separate small bowl, dissolve 1/4 teaspoon of active dry yeast in 1 cup of warm water.
> Add the yeast mixture to the dry ingredients and mix to form a rough dough. Turn the dough out onto a floured surface and knead for about 10-12 minutes until it becomes smooth and elastic. Add more flour if necessary to prevent sticking.

Place the kneaded dough in a lightly oiled bowl, cover with a kitchen towel, and let it rise in a warm place until doubled in size. This usually takes about 1-2 hours.

Once the dough has risen, gently punch it down and shape it into a round or oval loaf.

Place the shaped dough on a floured surface or in a proofing basket, cover it with a kitchen towel, and let it rise for another 45 minutes to 1 hour.

Preheat your oven to 450°F (232°C). If you have a baking stone, place it in the oven to heat.

If you're using a baking stone, carefully transfer the risen dough onto the hot stone. Alternatively, place the shaped dough on a parchment-lined baking sheet. Score the top of the dough with a sharp knife or razor.

Bake in the preheated oven for about 25-30 minutes or until the crust is golden brown and the bread sounds hollow when tapped on the bottom.

Allow the Country Bread to cool on a wire rack before slicing.

Enjoy your homemade Chleb Wiejski! This rustic country bread is perfect for sandwiches, toasting, or serving alongside your favorite meals.

**Bułki Płatki Owsiane (Oat Rolls)**

Ingredients:

- 2 cups all-purpose flour
- 1 cup rolled oats (oat flakes)
- 1/4 cup unsalted butter, softened
- 1 tablespoon honey or maple syrup
- 1 teaspoon salt
- 1 packet (2 1/4 teaspoons) active dry yeast
- 1 cup warm milk (about 110°F or 43°C)
- Additional rolled oats for topping (optional)

Instructions:

In a small bowl, combine warm milk, honey (or maple syrup), and active dry yeast. Let it sit for about 5-10 minutes until it becomes frothy.
In a large mixing bowl, combine all-purpose flour, rolled oats, softened butter, and salt.
Make a well in the center of the flour mixture. Pour in the activated yeast mixture. Mix the ingredients until a dough forms.
Turn the dough out onto a floured surface and knead for about 8-10 minutes until it becomes smooth and elastic. If the dough is too sticky, add additional flour as needed.
Place the kneaded dough in a greased bowl, cover it with a kitchen towel, and let it rise in a warm place until doubled in size. This usually takes about 1-2 hours.
Preheat your oven to 375°F (190°C).
Punch down the risen dough and turn it out onto a floured surface.
Divide the dough into equal portions to form rolls. Shape each portion into a round or oval shape.
Place the shaped rolls on a parchment-lined baking sheet, leaving some space between them.
Optionally, brush the tops of the rolls with a bit of milk and sprinkle additional rolled oats on top for a decorative touch.
Bake in the preheated oven for about 15-20 minutes or until the rolls are golden brown.
Allow the Oat Rolls to cool on a wire rack before serving.

Enjoy your homemade Bułki Płatki Owsiane! These oat rolls are perfect for breakfast, sandwiches, or as a side to complement various dishes.

**Chleb Razowy (Rye Bread)**

Ingredients:

- 2 cups rye flour
- 2 cups bread flour (or all-purpose flour)
- 1 1/2 teaspoons salt
- 1 tablespoon caraway seeds (optional, for added flavor)
- 1 packet (2 1/4 teaspoons) active dry yeast
- 1 tablespoon honey or molasses (optional, for sweetness)
- 1 1/2 cups warm water (about 110°F or 43°C)

Instructions:

> In a small bowl, combine warm water, honey (or molasses), and active dry yeast. Let it sit for about 5-10 minutes until it becomes frothy.
> In a large mixing bowl, combine rye flour, bread flour (or all-purpose flour), salt, and caraway seeds (if using).
> Make a well in the center of the flour mixture. Pour in the activated yeast mixture. Mix the ingredients until a dough forms.
> Turn the dough out onto a floured surface and knead for about 10-12 minutes until it becomes smooth and elastic. Add more flour if necessary to prevent sticking.
> Place the kneaded dough in a greased bowl, cover it with a kitchen towel, and let it rise in a warm place until doubled in size. This usually takes about 1-2 hours.
> Preheat your oven to 375°F (190°C).
> Punch down the risen dough and shape it into a round or oval loaf.
> Place the shaped dough on a parchment-lined baking sheet.
> Optionally, you can slash the top of the loaf with a sharp knife or razor for decorative purposes.
> Bake in the preheated oven for about 30-40 minutes or until the bread is golden brown and sounds hollow when tapped on the bottom.
> Allow the Rye Bread to cool on a wire rack before slicing.

Enjoy your homemade Chleb Razowy! This traditional Polish rye bread is perfect for sandwiches, toasting, or serving with soups and stews.

## Chałka (Sweet Bread)

Ingredients:

For the Dough:

- 4 to 4 1/2 cups all-purpose flour
- 1/2 cup granulated sugar
- 1 packet (2 1/4 teaspoons) active dry yeast
- 1 cup warm milk (about 110°F or 43°C)
- 1/2 cup unsalted butter, softened
- 3 large eggs
- 1 teaspoon vanilla extract
- 1/2 teaspoon salt

For the Egg Wash:

- 1 egg, beaten

Optional Toppings:

- Sesame seeds or poppy seeds

Instructions:

Prepare the Dough:

In a small bowl, combine warm milk, a pinch of sugar, and active dry yeast. Let it sit for about 5-10 minutes until it becomes frothy.
In a large mixing bowl, combine 4 cups of all-purpose flour, sugar, and salt.
Make a well in the center of the flour mixture. Pour in the activated yeast mixture, softened butter, eggs, and vanilla extract.
Mix the ingredients until a soft dough forms.
Knead the dough on a floured surface for about 10 minutes until it becomes smooth and elastic. If the dough is too sticky, add additional flour as needed.
Place the kneaded dough in a greased bowl, cover it with a kitchen towel, and let it rise in a warm place until doubled in size. This usually takes about 1-2 hours.

Shape and Bake:

Preheat your oven to 375°F (190°C). Line a baking sheet with parchment paper.
Punch down the risen dough and turn it out onto a floured surface.
Divide the dough into three equal parts. Roll each part into a long rope.

Braid the three ropes together, pinching the ends to seal.

Place the braided dough on the prepared baking sheet.

In a small bowl, beat an egg to create an egg wash. Brush the egg wash over the top of the braided dough.

Optionally, sprinkle sesame seeds or poppy seeds over the egg wash.

Bake in the preheated oven for about 25-30 minutes or until the bread is golden brown.

Allow the Chałka to cool on a wire rack before slicing.

Enjoy your homemade Chałka! This sweet braided bread is a beautiful addition to festive meals and celebrations.

**Bułki Pyszne (Delicious Rolls)**

Ingredients:

- 4 cups all-purpose flour
- 1 tablespoon sugar
- 1 teaspoon salt
- 1 packet (2 1/4 teaspoons) active dry yeast
- 1 cup warm milk (about 110°F or 43°C)
- 1/4 cup unsalted butter, melted
- 1 large egg

Instructions:

In a small bowl, combine warm milk, sugar, and active dry yeast. Let it sit for about 5-10 minutes until it becomes frothy.
In a large mixing bowl, combine 4 cups of all-purpose flour and salt.
Make a well in the center of the flour mixture. Pour in the activated yeast mixture, melted butter, and a beaten egg.
Mix the ingredients until a soft dough forms.
Turn the dough out onto a floured surface and knead for about 8-10 minutes until it becomes smooth and elastic. If the dough is too sticky, add additional flour as needed.
Place the kneaded dough in a greased bowl, cover it with a kitchen towel, and let it rise in a warm place until doubled in size. This usually takes about 1-2 hours.
Preheat your oven to 375°F (190°C). Line a baking sheet with parchment paper.
Punch down the risen dough and turn it out onto a floured surface.
Divide the dough into equal portions and shape each portion into a round roll.
Place the rolls on the prepared baking sheet, leaving some space between them.
Cover the rolls with a kitchen towel and let them rise for another 30-45 minutes.
Bake in the preheated oven for about 15-20 minutes or until the rolls are golden brown.
Allow the Delicious Rolls to cool on a wire rack before serving.

Feel free to customize these rolls by adding seeds, herbs, or any other ingredients you prefer. Enjoy your homemade delicious rolls!

## Bułki z Makiem (Poppy Seed Rolls)

Ingredients:

For the Dough:

- 3 cups all-purpose flour
- 1/2 cup sugar
- 1 packet (2 1/4 teaspoons) active dry yeast
- 1 cup warm milk (about 110°F or 43°C)
- 1/2 cup unsalted butter, melted
- 2 large eggs
- 1 teaspoon vanilla extract
- 1/2 teaspoon salt

For the Poppy Seed Filling:

- 1 cup ground poppy seeds
- 1/2 cup honey or sugar (adjust to taste)
- 1/2 cup milk
- 1/4 cup unsalted butter
- 1/4 cup chopped nuts (walnuts or almonds), optional
- Zest of 1 lemon or orange
- 1/2 teaspoon vanilla extract

Instructions:

Prepare the Dough:

> In a small bowl, combine warm milk, a pinch of sugar, and active dry yeast. Let it sit for about 5-10 minutes until it becomes frothy.
> In a large mixing bowl, combine 3 cups of all-purpose flour, sugar, and salt.
> Make a well in the center of the flour mixture. Pour in the activated yeast mixture, melted butter, eggs, and vanilla extract.
> Mix the ingredients until a soft dough forms.
> Turn the dough out onto a floured surface and knead for about 8-10 minutes until it becomes smooth and elastic. If the dough is too sticky, add additional flour as needed.
> Place the kneaded dough in a greased bowl, cover it with a kitchen towel, and let it rise in a warm place until doubled in size. This usually takes about 1-2 hours.

Prepare the Poppy Seed Filling:

In a saucepan, combine ground poppy seeds, honey (or sugar), milk, butter, chopped nuts (if using), lemon or orange zest, and vanilla extract.

Cook the mixture over low to medium heat, stirring constantly, until it thickens. This usually takes about 10-15 minutes.

Allow the poppy seed filling to cool.

Assemble the Poppy Seed Rolls:

Preheat your oven to 350°F (180°C). Line a baking sheet with parchment paper.

Punch down the risen dough and turn it out onto a floured surface.

Roll out the dough into a rectangle.

Spread the cooled poppy seed filling evenly over the dough.

Roll up the dough tightly from one of the longer sides to form a log.

Slice the log into individual rolls and place them on the prepared baking sheet.

Bake in the preheated oven for about 20-25 minutes or until the rolls are golden brown.

Allow the Poppy Seed Rolls to cool on a wire rack before serving.

Enjoy your Bułki z Makiem! These poppy seed rolls are a sweet and flavorful treat, perfect for breakfast or dessert.

## Chleb Pszenno-Zytni (Wheat-Rye Bread)

Ingredients:

For the Starter (Poolish):

- 1 cup bread flour
- 1/2 cup rye flour
- 1 cup warm water
- 1/4 teaspoon active dry yeast

For the Dough:

- All of the starter (poolish) from the previous step
- 2 cups bread flour
- 1 cup rye flour
- 1 1/2 teaspoons salt
- 1 tablespoon molasses or honey (optional, for sweetness)
- 1 1/4 cups warm water
- 1 packet (2 1/4 teaspoons) active dry yeast

Instructions:

Prepare the Starter (Poolish):

> In a bowl, combine 1 cup of bread flour, 1/2 cup of rye flour, 1 cup of warm water, and 1/4 teaspoon of active dry yeast.
> Mix until well combined. Cover the bowl with plastic wrap and let it sit at room temperature for at least 8 hours or overnight. This is your poolish starter.

Make the Dough:

> In a large mixing bowl, combine the poolish starter, 2 cups of bread flour, 1 cup of rye flour, salt, and molasses or honey (if using).
> In a separate small bowl, dissolve 1 packet of active dry yeast in 1 1/4 cups of warm water.
> Add the yeast mixture to the dry ingredients and mix to form a rough dough.
> Turn the dough out onto a floured surface and knead for about 10-12 minutes until it becomes smooth and elastic. Add more flour if necessary to prevent sticking.

Place the kneaded dough in a greased bowl, cover it with a kitchen towel, and let it rise in a warm place until doubled in size. This usually takes about 1-2 hours. Once the dough has risen, gently punch it down and shape it into a round or oval loaf.

Place the shaped dough in a proofing basket or on a parchment-lined baking sheet.

Cover the dough with a kitchen towel and let it rise for another 45 minutes to 1 hour.

Preheat your oven to 375°F (190°C).

If you're using a proofing basket, carefully transfer the risen dough onto a parchment-lined baking sheet. Alternatively, place the shaped dough directly on the parchment-lined baking sheet.

Optionally, slash the top of the loaf with a sharp knife or razor for decorative purposes.

Bake in the preheated oven for about 30-40 minutes or until the bread is golden brown and sounds hollow when tapped on the bottom.

Allow the Wheat-Rye Bread to cool on a wire rack before slicing.

Enjoy your homemade Chleb Pszenno-Zytni! This wheat-rye bread is perfect for sandwiches, toasting, or serving alongside soups and stews.

**Bułki Drożdżowe (Yeast Rolls)**

Ingredients:

- 4 cups all-purpose flour
- 1/4 cup granulated sugar
- 1 packet (2 1/4 teaspoons) active dry yeast
- 1 cup warm milk (about 110°F or 43°C)
- 1/4 cup unsalted butter, melted
- 1 teaspoon salt
- 2 large eggs

Instructions:

In a small bowl, combine warm milk, sugar, and active dry yeast. Let it sit for about 5-10 minutes until it becomes frothy.
In a large mixing bowl, combine 4 cups of all-purpose flour and salt.
Make a well in the center of the flour mixture. Pour in the activated yeast mixture, melted butter, and eggs.
Mix the ingredients until a soft dough forms.
Turn the dough out onto a floured surface and knead for about 8-10 minutes until it becomes smooth and elastic. If the dough is too sticky, add additional flour as needed.
Place the kneaded dough in a greased bowl, cover it with a kitchen towel, and let it rise in a warm place until doubled in size. This usually takes about 1-2 hours.
Preheat your oven to 375°F (190°C). Line a baking sheet with parchment paper.
Punch down the risen dough and turn it out onto a floured surface.
Divide the dough into equal portions and shape each portion into a round roll.
Place the rolls on the prepared baking sheet, leaving some space between them.
Cover the rolls with a kitchen towel and let them rise for another 30-45 minutes.
Bake in the preheated oven for about 15-20 minutes or until the rolls are golden brown.
Allow the Yeast Rolls to cool on a wire rack before serving.

These Bułki Drożdżowe can be served with butter and jam for breakfast, used as sandwich rolls, or enjoyed as a side with meals. Customize them by adding seeds, herbs, or other ingredients according to your preference. Enjoy your homemade yeast rolls!

## Chleb Ziemniaczany (Potato Bread)

Ingredients:

For the Potato Mash:

- 2 large potatoes, peeled and diced
- Water for boiling
- Salt

For the Bread Dough:

- 1 1/2 cups warm milk (about 110°F or 43°C)
- 1 tablespoon active dry yeast
- 1/4 cup granulated sugar
- 1/4 cup unsalted butter, melted
- 1 teaspoon salt
- 4 to 4 1/2 cups all-purpose flour
- 1 cup cooled mashed potatoes (prepared from the earlier step)

Instructions:

Prepare the Potato Mash:

> Peel and dice the potatoes.
> Boil the diced potatoes in salted water until they are tender.
> Drain the potatoes and mash them until smooth. Let the mashed potatoes cool to room temperature.

Make the Bread Dough:

> In a small bowl, combine warm milk, sugar, and active dry yeast. Let it sit for about 5-10 minutes until it becomes frothy.
> In a large mixing bowl, combine 4 cups of all-purpose flour and salt.
> Make a well in the center of the flour mixture. Pour in the activated yeast mixture, melted butter, and cooled mashed potatoes.
> Mix the ingredients until a soft dough forms.
> Turn the dough out onto a floured surface and knead for about 8-10 minutes until it becomes smooth and elastic. Add additional flour as needed to prevent sticking.
> Place the kneaded dough in a greased bowl, cover it with a kitchen towel, and let it rise in a warm place until doubled in size. This usually takes about 1-2 hours.
> Preheat your oven to 375°F (190°C). Grease a bread pan.

Punch down the risen dough and shape it into a loaf. Place the shaped dough in the prepared bread pan.
Cover the pan with a kitchen towel and let the dough rise for another 30-45 minutes.
Bake in the preheated oven for about 30-40 minutes or until the bread is golden brown and sounds hollow when tapped on the bottom.
Allow the Potato Bread to cool in the pan for a few minutes before transferring it to a wire rack to cool completely.

Enjoy your homemade Chleb Ziemniaczany! This potato bread is wonderful for sandwiches, toasting, or serving with soups and stews. The addition of mashed potatoes adds a unique and delicious element to the bread.

## Bułki Cynamonowe (Cinnamon Rolls)

Ingredients:

For the Dough:

- 4 cups all-purpose flour
- 1/3 cup granulated sugar
- 1 packet (2 1/4 teaspoons) active dry yeast
- 1 cup warm milk (about 110°F or 43°C)
- 1/4 cup unsalted butter, melted
- 1/2 teaspoon salt
- 2 large eggs

For the Filling:

- 1/2 cup unsalted butter, softened
- 1 cup brown sugar, packed
- 2 tablespoons ground cinnamon

For the Cream Cheese Frosting:

- 4 oz (about 1/2 cup) cream cheese, softened
- 1/4 cup unsalted butter, softened
- 1 cup powdered sugar
- 1/2 teaspoon vanilla extract
- A pinch of salt

Instructions:

Prepare the Dough:

> In a small bowl, combine warm milk, sugar, and active dry yeast. Let it sit for about 5-10 minutes until it becomes frothy.
> In a large mixing bowl, combine 4 cups of all-purpose flour and salt.
> Make a well in the center of the flour mixture. Pour in the activated yeast mixture, melted butter, and eggs.
> Mix the ingredients until a soft dough forms.
> Turn the dough out onto a floured surface and knead for about 8-10 minutes until it becomes smooth and elastic. Add more flour if necessary to prevent sticking.

Place the kneaded dough in a greased bowl, cover it with a kitchen towel, and let it rise in a warm place until doubled in size. This usually takes about 1-2 hours.

Make the Filling:

In a small bowl, mix together the softened butter, brown sugar, and ground cinnamon to create the filling.

Assemble and Bake:

Preheat your oven to 375°F (190°C). Grease a baking dish.
Punch down the risen dough and turn it out onto a floured surface.
Roll out the dough into a rectangle.
Spread the cinnamon-sugar filling evenly over the dough.
Starting from one of the longer sides, tightly roll up the dough to form a log.
Slice the log into individual rolls and place them in the prepared baking dish.
Bake in the preheated oven for about 20-25 minutes or until the rolls are golden brown.

Make the Cream Cheese Frosting:

In a bowl, beat together softened cream cheese, butter, powdered sugar, vanilla extract, and a pinch of salt until smooth.
Once the cinnamon rolls have cooled slightly, spread the cream cheese frosting over the top.

Enjoy your homemade Bułki Cynamonowe! These cinnamon rolls are best served warm and are a delightful treat for any occasion.

# Polish Beverages:

**Kompot Owocowy (Fruit Compote)**

Ingredients:

- 4 cups mixed fruits (such as apples, pears, peaches, berries, or any fruits of your choice), peeled and chopped
- 1/2 cup sugar (adjust to taste)
- 6 cups water
- 1 cinnamon stick (optional)
- 3-4 cloves (optional)
- 1-2 tablespoons lemon juice (optional)

Instructions:

Prepare the Fruits:
- Wash, peel (if needed), and chop the fruits into bite-sized pieces.

Cooking the Compote:
- In a large pot, combine the chopped fruits, sugar, and water.
- If using, add a cinnamon stick and cloves for added flavor.
- Bring the mixture to a boil over medium heat.

Simmering:
- Once boiling, reduce the heat to low and let the fruit mixture simmer for about 15-20 minutes or until the fruits are tender.

Adjusting Sweetness:
- Taste the compote and adjust the sweetness by adding more sugar if necessary. Stir until the sugar dissolves.

Optional Additions:
- If you like a bit of tartness, you can add 1-2 tablespoons of lemon juice. Adjust according to your preference.

Cooling:
- Remove the pot from heat and let the fruit compote cool to room temperature.

Chilling (Optional):
- Refrigerate the compote for a few hours before serving if you prefer it cold.

Serve:

- Serve the Fruit Compote in glasses or bowls, including some of the fruit pieces in each serving.

Garnish (Optional):
- Garnish with fresh mint leaves or a slice of lemon if desired.

Enjoy your homemade Kompot Owocowy! This versatile fruit compote can be served as a refreshing beverage, a light dessert, or even poured over ice cream. It's a delightful way to enjoy the natural sweetness of various fruits.

**Kisiel (Fruit Jelly)**

Ingredients:

- 1 cup fruit juice (such as raspberry, cherry, blackcurrant, or any fruit juice of your choice)
- 3-4 tablespoons sugar (adjust to taste)
- 3 tablespoons potato starch or cornstarch
- 1/2 cup cold water

Instructions:

Prepare the Starch Mixture:
- In a small bowl, dissolve the potato starch or cornstarch in cold water, creating a smooth mixture. Ensure there are no lumps.

Heat the Fruit Juice:
- In a saucepan, heat the fruit juice over medium heat until it starts to simmer. Add sugar to the juice and stir until it dissolves.

Thicken the Juice:
- Once the juice is simmering, gradually pour the starch mixture into the saucepan while stirring continuously to avoid lumps.

Simmering:
- Continue to simmer the mixture, stirring constantly, until it thickens to a pudding-like consistency. This usually takes about 5-7 minutes.

Adjust Sweetness:
- Taste the Kisiel and adjust the sweetness by adding more sugar if needed. Stir until the sugar dissolves.

Cooling:
- Remove the saucepan from heat and let the Kisiel cool to room temperature.

Chilling (Optional):
- You can refrigerate the Kisiel for a few hours if you prefer it served cold.

Serve:
- Serve the Fruit Jelly in individual bowls or glasses.

Garnish (Optional):
- Garnish with fresh berries, mint leaves, or a dollop of whipped cream if desired.

Enjoy your homemade Kisiel! This simple and refreshing fruit jelly is a delightful dessert, and its flavor can be customized based on your choice of fruit juice.

## Wódka (Vodka)

Production:

> Ingredients: Vodka is typically made from fermented grains or potatoes, though it can be produced from other sources like fruits or sugar.
> Fermentation: The raw ingredients are fermented to produce alcohol. The resulting liquid is then distilled to increase its alcohol content.
> Distillation: Vodka undergoes multiple distillations to achieve a high level of purity. It is distilled at a high proof to remove impurities and flavors.
> Filtering: Some vodka brands may use additional processes such as filtration through charcoal to further refine and purify the spirit.

Characteristics:

- Neutral Flavor: Vodka is known for its neutral taste, allowing it to serve as a base for a wide variety of cocktails.
- Alcohol Content: Vodka typically has a high alcohol by volume (ABV) percentage, usually ranging from 40% to 50%.
- Clarity: Vodka is usually clear and colorless. Flavored vodkas may have a slight hue depending on the added ingredients.

Serving:

- Chilled: Vodka is often served chilled or over ice to enhance its smoothness.
- Cocktails: It is a key ingredient in numerous cocktails, such as the Martini, Moscow Mule, Bloody Mary, and Cosmopolitan.
- Straight: Some people prefer to drink vodka neat or straight.

Popular Brands:

- Belvedere
- Chopin
- Wyborowa
- Żubrówka (known for its bison grass flavor)
- Luksusowa (made from potatoes)

Note:

- It's important to consume alcoholic beverages responsibly and be aware of the legal drinking age in your location.

Whether enjoyed on its own or as part of a cocktail, vodka is a versatile spirit that has become a global favorite. Keep in mind that the production methods and characteristics of vodka can vary among brands and regions.

## Herbata (Tea)

Types of Tea:

- Black Tea: Fully oxidized tea leaves, resulting in a robust flavor. Common varieties include English Breakfast and Earl Grey.
- Green Tea: Unoxidized tea leaves, retaining a more delicate flavor. Sencha and matcha are popular green tea varieties.
- Herbal Tea: Made from dried fruits, flowers, herbs, or spices, not technically tea leaves. Examples include chamomile, peppermint, and fruit infusions.
- White Tea: Minimal processing, with leaves harvested at an early stage. White tea has a delicate flavor and subtle aroma.
- Oolong Tea: Partially oxidized tea leaves, falling between green and black tea. It offers a range of flavors from floral to fruity.

Polish Tea Culture:

- Herbata z Cytryną (Tea with Lemon): A common way to enjoy tea in Poland is with a slice of lemon. It adds a citrusy flavor and is often served with sugar.
- Herbata z Miodem (Tea with Honey): Honey is a popular sweetener for tea, providing a natural and soothing sweetness.
- Herbata z Malinami (Tea with Raspberries): During the cold months, a warm cup of tea with raspberries or raspberry jam is a comforting choice.

Tea Drinking Rituals:

- Afternoon Tea: Some people in Poland enjoy a cup of tea in the afternoon, often accompanied by biscuits, pastries, or sandwiches.
- Herbata na Zdrowie (Tea for Health): Herbal teas are often chosen for their perceived health benefits. Popular choices include mint tea for digestion or chamomile tea for relaxation.
- Ceremonial Tea: While not as formalized as in some cultures, Poles may share a cup of tea during social gatherings, offering a moment for conversation and connection.

Brands:

While Poland is known for its love of coffee, tea is also appreciated. Various international and local brands offer a wide selection of teas to suit different tastes.

Note:

Tea is a versatile beverage enjoyed in various ways around the world. Whether you prefer it hot or cold, with added flavors or in its pure form, tea offers a comforting and social drinking experience.

## Kawa (Coffee)

Coffee Types:

> Kawa Czarna (Black Coffee): Simple black coffee is a popular choice. It can be served as espresso (mała czarna) or as a longer black coffee (duża czarna).
> Kawa z Mlekiem (Coffee with Milk): Adding milk to coffee is common. You can have a latte (kawa biała) with more milk or a smaller amount of milk in a coffee (kawa z mlekiem).
> Kawa Zbożowa (Barley Coffee): A caffeine-free alternative made from roasted barley, providing a coffee-like flavor.
> Kawa Rozpuszczalna (Instant Coffee): Instant coffee is convenient and widely used. It's often served with sugar and powdered creamer.

Coffee Culture:

> Kawiarnia (Coffeehouse): Polish cities have numerous coffeehouses where people gather to enjoy coffee, desserts, and socialize. Cafés often have a cozy atmosphere.
> Kawa na Wynos (Takeaway Coffee): Like in many places, Polish people often grab a coffee to go, especially during busy mornings.
> Kawa z Zaparzaczem (Pour-Over Coffee): Some coffee enthusiasts appreciate pour-over coffee made with high-quality beans. Specialty coffee shops offer various brewing methods.

Traditional Coffee Drinks:

> Kawa po Turecku (Turkish Coffee): A strong, unfiltered coffee brewed with finely ground coffee beans, sugar, and water. It's often served in a small cup.
> Kawa Parzona (Boiled Coffee): Coarsely ground coffee is boiled with water and sometimes sugar. It's a traditional method, particularly in rural areas.

Popular Brands:

Woseba: A well-known Polish coffee brand offering various blends.
Jacobs: A German coffee brand popular in Poland, offering a range of coffee products.
Tchibo: A German brand with a significant presence in Poland, providing a variety of coffee blends.

Note:

Poland has a strong coffee culture, but tea is also widely enjoyed. Whether you prefer a quick espresso, a leisurely latte, or a traditional Turkish coffee, you can find a variety of coffee options to suit your taste in Poland.

## Kefir (Fermented Milk Drink)

Key Characteristics:

Fermentation Process: Kefir is made through the fermentation of milk with kefir grains, which are small, gelatinous clusters of bacteria and yeast. The fermentation process results in a thick, tangy, and effervescent beverage.
Probiotic Content: Kefir is rich in probiotics, which are beneficial microorganisms that can contribute to gut health. These probiotics include various strains of bacteria and yeast.
Taste and Texture: The flavor of kefir is tangy and slightly sour, and its consistency can range from liquid to a more yogurt-like thickness. Some varieties may have a natural effervescence.
Nutritional Benefits: Kefir is a good source of several nutrients, including protein, calcium, and B vitamins. Additionally, its probiotic content may support digestive health.

Serving and Consumption:

Plain Kefir: Plain kefir is commonly consumed as is, either chilled or at room temperature.
Flavored Varieties: Commercially available kefir often comes in various flavors such as strawberry, mango, or vanilla. These flavored versions can be more appealing to those who prefer a sweeter taste.
Smoothies: Kefir is a popular ingredient in smoothies, adding a tangy flavor and nutritional boost.

Making Kefir at Home:

Ingredients:
- Kefir grains
- Milk (cow's milk, goat's milk, or non-dairy alternatives like coconut or almond milk)

Instructions:
- Place the kefir grains in a glass jar.
- Add milk to the jar, leaving some space at the top.
- Cover the jar with a cloth or paper towel and secure it with a rubber band.
- Allow the mixture to ferment at room temperature for about 12 to 48 hours, depending on desired thickness and flavor.
- Strain out the kefir grains and transfer the liquid to another container.

- Refrigerate the kefir before consuming.

Note:

- Kefir grains can be obtained from someone who already makes kefir or purchased online. They are reusable and can be used to ferment multiple batches of kefir.

Kefir is not only a refreshing beverage but also a probiotic-rich food that can be a valuable addition to a balanced diet. It's a versatile drink that can be enjoyed in various ways based on personal preferences.

**Piwo (Beer)**

Types of Beer:

    Piwo Jasne (Pale Lager): The most popular type of beer in Poland. It is a light, golden-colored lager with a mild flavor. Brands like Tyskie and Żywiec are well-known.
    Piwo Ciemne (Dark Lager): A darker and richer beer with roasted malt flavors. It has a more pronounced caramel or chocolate taste. Brands like Okocim Porter fall into this category.
    Piwo Pszeniczne (Wheat Beer): Brewed with a significant proportion of wheat, giving it a hazy appearance and a light, refreshing taste. Brands like Żywiec Białe fall into this category.
    Piwo Craftowe (Craft Beer): The craft beer movement has gained popularity in Poland, leading to the production of various artisanal and unique beer styles with diverse flavors.
    Piwo Miodowe (Honey Beer): Some breweries produce beer with added honey for a touch of sweetness. It's a niche but appreciated category.

Beer Culture:

    Pubs and Beer Gardens: Pubs and outdoor beer gardens (piwiarnie or piwiarnie ogrodowe) are popular places for socializing and enjoying beer.
    Beer Festivals: Poland hosts various beer festivals where breweries showcase their products. These events often include a variety of beer styles, including craft beers.
    Food Pairing: Beer is often enjoyed with traditional Polish dishes, including grilled meats, sausages, and pierogi.

Brands:

    Tyskie: One of the oldest breweries in Poland, known for its pale lager.
    Żywiec: A well-known brewery producing a range of beer styles.
    Okocim: Famous for its dark lager and other beer varieties.
    Lech: Another popular Polish brewery offering a variety of beers.
    Browar Namysłów: Representing the craft beer movement with a range of artisanal brews.

Craft Beer Revolution:

The craft beer scene in Poland has seen significant growth in recent years, with many microbreweries and craft beer bars emerging. Craft brewers experiment with various ingredients and brewing techniques, offering beer enthusiasts a diverse range of flavors and styles.

Note:

Poland has a rich beer culture with a variety of beer styles to suit different preferences. Whether enjoying a traditional pale lager in a local pub or exploring unique craft brews at a beer festival, piwo plays a significant role in socializing and culinary experiences.